Janice Barnett Ged Palmer Jo Simpson



# They Thought It Was All Over

## ...they were right!

What the England Football team needs to know in order to win the World Cup

ecademyPRESS

Cover Design, Book Design and Typesetting by **Ayd Instone**
Set in *Stone Sans* on 9pt

First published in 2010 by:

**Ecademy Press**

48 St Vincent Drive, St Albans, Herts, AL1 5SJ
info@ecademy-press.com • www.ecademy-press.com

Printed and Bound by:
Lightning Source in the UK and USA

Printed on acid-free paper from managed forests. This book is printed on demand, so no copies will be remaindered or pulped.

ISBN-978-1-905823-79-6



*A CIP catalogue record for this book is available from the British Library.*

# Contents

# Foreword

This is a book born of passion. All three of us are passionate about getting the best from people and are passionate about our football. It seemed natural to combine these two passions in one book and celebrate our shared values of Fun, Dedication, Challenge, Contribution and Discovery.

## How it all started

It all started on the night of 1st July 2006 in Double Decker's bar, Dubai, the night England exited the World Cup after their penalty shootout against Portugal. Standing among the several thousand who had gathered in the hastily erected marquee to watch the match, Jo and Janice couldn't help but notice the negativity of both the crowd and the match commentators in relation to England's abilities and the likelihood of their success. This negativity appeared to have transferred to the players who seemed defeated long before they were.

Emerging into the night "We never win on penalties" still ringing in their ears, a sinking feeling in their hearts, sick at the way England's World Cup run had turned out (again) and angry at the lack of faith from the crowd, Jo and Janice decided that enough was enough and vowed to do something to stimulate a positive approach to football throughout the nation.

After discussing the self-fulfilling prophecy that surrounded the team and its media coverage with Ged, our search commenced to find answers to why the England team had performed below expectations and to find solutions to correct this. We believe that a change of mindset among all those involved in the English game, fans included, is the answer. This current mindset, which serves no-one, is summed up perfectly below in a blog entry from 'thedisintegrator':

"You can't win when you don't have that winning mentality. England will have to get it into their heads that they are one of the best teams in the world, worthy of respect and to be feared. Just look at the likes of Brazil and Italy. They don't have to say it because they already know it. We're Brazil, we're Italy, respect and fear us. That is the message. England gives out the "We're England" and that's where it ends. We need a manager to give us that mentality. There are no more excuses, the players are there, what's missing is that mentality".

Our solutions are now recorded here for your enlightenment. We've focused mainly on the events, team and personalities of the 2006 World Cup yet the wisdom in these pages can be applied, and indeed should be applied, in a much broader context. Visions for a glorious footballing future should start on the school playing field if not in the street or back garden.

Whilst we've drawn from newspapers, TV, internet, blog sites (giving credit wherever possible) and from listening to and joining in with post competition debate, we have also taken some liberties and allowed personal speculation and creative thinking to enter these pages. This is our take on how things are – we don't have all the answers yet we believe we offer a genuine set of solutions.

# How do we want this book to be used?

First and foremost we hope this book will entertain you, generate debate, provoke thought and stir discussions. It is designed to provide insight to what went wrong and how the situation can be turned around.

Our book was written during the immediate aftermath of the FIFA World Cup in Germany 2006 and, as such, it reflects a time and a place and a particular mood amongst the players, fans, media, and the English public. We realise that things have moved on since then. At the time of publication, we are now in the brave 'back-to-basics' world of Fabio Cappello after the torrid and inept interregnum of Steve McClaren under which England suffered further humiliation in not even qualifying for the European Nations Championships in 2008. With the passing of time, some of the 'names' and the parts they played in the high drama of Germany 2006 may already have faded from our consciousness, bad memories almost as unappetising as a pre-season Inter-Toto friendly. In addition, it would be too hazardous to guess as to which players will survive the 'reconstruction' that has already begun and who will still be playing for England by the time the next World Cup comes around.

In inviting the reader to relive the events of England's 2006 World Cup campaign and our untimely exit, our intention is not to take some sadistic and vicarious pleasure in conjuring up the abject misery and disappointment that was so keenly felt by many at the time.

Our intention is to draw out lessons from the facts and illustrate how things could be different. This book is about breaking patterns, not wallowing in the continual cycle of unfulfilled promise, despair and disillusionment which some would have us believe is, and will always be, the permanent state of our beloved national game.

Leaving aside the context of World Cup 2006, we believe that in sifting through the details of England's (and others') performances both on and off the pitch, clues can be found as to why England chronically underachieve in major tournaments while others excel. These are lessons that need to be taken on board if we are to see English football reclaim its rightful place at the top of the World Rankings.

Our proposition is that only by adopting radical change in their approach will sustainable outstanding results be achieved. We aim to inspire belief in a positive future for the England team. The messages in these pages may also be applied beyond the football world – these are life skills that can serve in any arena.

We have had a bit of fun with a couple of the chapters (hopefully you'll be able to work out which ones!). Great stories came out of the 2006 World Cup; some where lessons can be learned and others that are just bonkers. One of our favourite bizarre tales involves Noel (Oasis) Gallagher's pants: Italian striker Alessandro del Piero insisted that his friend and rock legend Noel Gallagher (who was following the Italian team, make of this what you will!) wear exactly the same clothes - and we're talking socks, underwear, the lot - for the Final as he had worn during the semi-Final for luck! (Hopefully there was time in between for a trip to the launderette).

This book is born of a genuine desire to deliver something positive and valuable. We believe there are many elements of the England team that make them great; we just want to "make them mightier yet."

## Thank you

Finally, many people have helped in the creation of this book (both knowingly and inadvertently). We would like to thank them for their time, support, comments and contributions:

To our wonderful editor (you know who you are) - for your attention to detail and tireless devotion to improving our spelling and grammar. To our many friends, who have given of their time and views and in particular to Geraldine Wynne for providing editorial comment and inspiration in the small hours; to the staff at the Lime Tree and MORE Cafes in Dubai for keeping us supplied with endless cups of tea and coffee and patiently tolerating our late departures.

In addition, we would like to thank our publishers, Ecademy Press, for providing the route to publication, Ayd Instone (www.sunmakers.co.uk) our designer, who came up with an innovative eye catching cover and page design and also to Gary Lineker for his quote and encouragement. Finally, Janice Barnett and Ged Palmer would like to make a special mention of the contribution of our fellow author, Jo Simpson, for never giving up on this project and steering our book through to successful publication.

# Chapter 1:
# Picture this...

## Soccer city
## Johannesburg, South Africa
## Sunday evening, July 11th 2010

For a moment, for that one jaw-dropping moment, there was nothing...

No sound, no colour, no form, no thought, no feeling, nothing... nada... rien... niente... neechto! The world had stopped breathing and stared open-mouthed, uncomprehending and dumb.

Only an image, glowing in the arc lights of the stadium, burning into the minds of the millions who were watching... the bulge in the net, the gloved hand, outstretched and grasping at air.

Then suddenly meaning descended and broke like a tropical rainstorm around the stadium. The air crackled with the electricity of realisation.

It was the moment of victory, the moment of truth, the moment that every footballer dreams of, the moment that every England fan had yearned for, THE moment that we would all remember for the rest of our lives...!!

Steven Gerrard turned away from the flashing scoreboard, England 5 - Spain 3, and fought back the tears of joy. His shot from the penalty spot had just won the World Cup for England.

It was all over!

Like a bolt of lightning, his arm jerked forward and up into the African night, pointing to the stars in triumph. Then he disappeared as his team mates, sprinting from the touchline in a wild gallop, buried him in a wriggling ball of frenzied joy. Their screams were just mimes of ecstasy, lost in the roar of the crowd, a roar which boomed and thundered and rolled around the terraces.

"England, England, England, E-N-G-L-A-N-D!"

"We ARE the Champions... of the World!"

On the terraces, draped with the banners of the England supporters clubs, exotic names in a foreign land: 'Billericay', 'Ashton-under-Lyme', 'The Lighthouse Pub Wallasey', 'Stapleford Old Boys', 'Hemel Hempstead', similar scenes of ecstasy broke out as thousands of fans cheered, clapped, sang, danced, wept, hugged each other - the same fans who had followed England from Rustenburg to Cape Town to Johannesburg in growing confidence and belief that this was their time, this was the team to do it, the 'golden generation' had finally come good on its promise and delivered.

"Football's coming home at last!"

Over the Tannoy system, an African voice announced that the Golden Boot Award would be shared between Wayne Rooney and Frank Lampard, the two outstanding players of the tournament, while Theo Walcott would be awarded the honour of top goal-scorer, beating all previous records set with his haul of 12 goals!

Wild applause cascaded around the field.

Then the rituals of victory began, celebrated in England colours of red and white - a scene to be savoured by the fans as if waking from a long-cherished but guiltily-imagined dream.

The laps of honour, the robotic and ridiculous Crouch dance by the squad, the shirt exchanges, scarves and outrageous banners from the crowds, the Three Lions rampant dancing on top of the world!

"Champions, Champions, C-H-A-M-P-I-O-N-S!"

The roar grows even louder and more expectant when, after a dignified interval of processional grace, jubilant members of the England squad line up to collect their winners' medals. The gold glints around their necks in the flash of the camera scrum. Tomorrow the world will breakfast on pictures of the victorious England Team members – arms around each other – broad grins now, relief and triumph written on their faces.

Over the loudspeakers music is playing to a live African drumbeat – it's an oldie but the song is strangely familiar "Diamonds on the soles of their shoes"...

Then dramatically, in a Euro-English accent, an announcement, quivering with emotion and excitement:

"And now Ladiez and Gentlemenn, I gif you the neuw Footboll Championz of de World – E n - g l a n d!"

The crowd draws breath.

On cue, the Presidents of South Africa and FIFA, coyly push the trophy forward on its podium. The England Captain steps up and grasps the FIFA World Cup and in one swift motion, raises it aloft as the tickertape bursts behind him in a riot of red and white...

The crowd erupts, the roar of 90,000 football fans shaking the very roof of the stadium and the TV cameras judder in weird synchrony.

The team passes the cup backwards and forwards –they all want to hold it, fondle it, kiss it, and caress it – the Holy Grail of football looking like a small toy, almost insignificant, in their hands.

The England Head Coach, balanced at a crazy angle on the shoulders of his team, cradles the Cup like a baby in his arms, before it is snatched from his grasp by Rio Ferdinand with a cheeky grin, then Gareth Barry pretends to drop it, before it is picked up between Joe Cole and the veteran David James, the hero of the penalty shootout.

The roar goes on and on and on and on.

"E-N-G-L-A-N-D, E-N-G-L-A-N-D, E-N-G-L-..."

## Chapter 2:

# It wasn't always so....

**Stansted Airport**
**England**
**Sunday afternoon, July 8th 2006**

When the British Airways jet touched down on the runway on the far side of the Airport, the small huddle of waiting fans who were gathered in the blistering heat at the perimeter fence realised they were to get no more than a fleeting glimpse of their returning 'heroes'.

It was the final let-down by Ericksson's men: the squad which had been so keen to pose for the cameras and sign autographs just three weeks before was now sitting on the runway, anxiously waiting for their chauffeur-driven cars to arrive and whisk them away to the privacy of their plush estates in the

Southern counties, hoping not to see or be seen, shut the world out, forget the nightmare ...

It was expecting too much for the Football Association to arrange a gesture of goodwill, for the players to sign a few more autographs and connect with the fans, many of whom had only wanted to commiserate in their grief and wish them "better luck, next time."

A young member of the England Supporters Club from Bishop Stortford said to a waiting reporter:

"There are not many of us here, but they should have come off the plane and signed autographs and posed for photos.

We are all as disappointed as they are.

They are sad – well the whole country is sad, people have been crying too and the players should have come back here to talk to us.

We had thousands of fans out in Germany, and we all thought this was going to be the year as well"

Enough said... the cars sped away from the runway while the jet with Rooney and the other northern players taxied and quickly took off again.

The players would creep away and hide, while a nation gathered its collective grief around it like a blanket and wallowed in yet another hard-luck, what-might-have-been. But would it be any different next time or, as one journalist (Jim van Wink of PA Sport) wrote, would we "no doubt see many more oh-so-nears which have now become part and parcel of the roller-coaster ride in following England since that balmy day at Wembley almost half a century ago."

To accept that prognosis of a repeating cycle of hope and despair would really be a defeat too far. Only a lunatic believes that by repeating the same behaviour again and again will you eventually get a different result.

But how can we break this cycle?

We contend that there is a way, there is an approach with a set of tools and techniques, which, when applied consistently, will radically change the performance of the national team, will prevent future failures and guarantee success in English World-Cup soccer.

Before we explain these ideas further let's take a look at the five matches of England's World Cup campaign…

## Chapter 3:

# Just not good enough...

**"But don't look back in anger, I hear you say"**

**– Noel Gallagher, Oasis**

As a light-hearted reminder of each of the England team's five games during the tournament in Germany 2006, our 'special correspondents' have pulled together some of the headlines and comments from the event. We invite you to relive the nightmare!

**England 1 Paraguay 0 10 June Frankfurt**

*From our correspondent in Frankfurt – Andy Owen Gole*

After their first game, against Paraguay in this World Cup, England will be delighted to be sitting at the top of Group B. England dominated for long periods and Gerrard delivered a disciplined performance but, beyond this, there was little cause for celebration.

England had to look to Paraguay to score on their behalf as Carlos Gamarra glanced a Beckham free kick into his own goal mouth just two minutes into the game.

Eriksson took Owen off in favour of Downing on 55 minutes and explained this move- "I thought we were finding it difficult to keep the ball so I tried to have a player who could link the ball up a little", a rare explanation of his often bewildering tactics.

England's fading performance was put down to the sizzling heat in the Frankfurt stadium, but, as one fan put it, "Beckham plays in Spain, what, they don't have hot weather there"?

Not the start we'd necessarily hoped for but three points nonetheless and England are bound to improve with time.

**England 2 Trinidad &Tobago 0 15 June Nuremburg**

*From our correspondent in Nuremburg – Faith Dwindling*

This was indeed a cruel result for Trinidad & Tobago, who were making their first appearance in a World Cup with a team made up of players mainly from the lower ranks of English league – Wrexham, Port Vale, Gillingham - and who had kept England at bay by their "gutsy performance" for 80 minutes.

With the England team misfiring and looking jittery, the chant from the crowd for Rooney began in earnest as early as 29 minutes into the game although they had to wait for the second half to get what they so dearly wanted. His appearance, however, was viewed by some as "a desperate last ditch gamble as England struggled to fire for the second game in succession".

Dwight Yorke came close to scoring in the 37th minute and England were startled into action.

Crouch and Lampard both missed golden opportunities before Crouch finally struck 7 minutes from time when he out-jumped a defender to head home a Beckham cross. Gerrard followed up on 90 minutes driving a powerful shot into the back of the net to ensure the result.

Despite England having 62% of the possession, and Crouch scoring his 6th goal in 5 internationals, England were booed off the field at half time by some sections of the crowd. Not a good sign. However, England are bound to improve with time.

**England 2 Sweden 2 20 June Cologne**

*From our correspondent in Cologne – Dee Fensive-Blunder*

Once again we chant the mantra of 1st half good, with the exception of loosing Owen to a twisted knee in the opening minute, 2nd half not so good. In a fast flowing game, Rooney was exuberant and Lampard enjoyed the freedom afforded him by having Hargreaves as his partner. Joe Cole managed to penetrate down the left flanks and scored a wonderful opening goal.

True to form, the second half saw a nervy performance and after Marcus Allback scored the Swedish 51st minute equalizer, the 2000th goal in World Cup history, England looked decidedly shaken.

Gerrard scored, from a Joe Cole cross, on 85 minutes putting England back into the lead. However, a defensive lapse by Sol Campbell saw Sweden equalize in the dying seconds of the game.

With Owen out for the rest of the tournament, the implication of Sven's decision to leave Jermaine Dafoe at home began to dawn.

A disappointing performance from Beckham, compounded by an equally dreary team performance, didn't bode well but at least we've avoided meeting Germany in the next round and England are bound to improve with time.

**England 1 Ecuador 0 25 June Stuttgart**

*From our correspondent in Stuttgart – Matt Chuggley*

Both England and Ecuador had chances to get on the score sheet during the first half. The best shot for England came from Lampard, one of two great scoring opportunities which he failed to convert, in the 27th minute, whilst Rooney and Gerrard both made attempts on goal. Ecuador's best chance of the first half was a miss-hit headed back pass from John Terry to Paul Robinson, which Carlos Tenorio was quick to pick up, his attempt only thwarted by a last ditch effort from Ashley Cole which deflected the ball onto the cross bar.

Beckham became the first player for England to score in three different World Cup competitions when he found the net with his typical, trademark free kick on

60 minutes. The excitement was obviously too much for him and he was taken off a short while later feeling unwell.

Despite what, according to Beckham "was an ugly performance but it is what we wanted and we will take ugly", England are through to the Quarter finals. Reporters, fans and players alike all remain certain that England are bound to improve with time

**England 0 (1) Portugal 0 (3) 1 July Gelsenkirchen**

*From our correspondent in Gelsenkirchen – Willy Stomp*

For once we were treated to a full 90 minutes of enthralling and captivating football despite the exit of Wayne Rooney. England provided the drama through sheer

force of determination and spirit, putting a climatic finish to the game when John Terry's shot was deflected just over the bar in the very last minute.

The Portuguese drama was more literal with displays of acting worthy of an Oscar. Plenty of diving, tripping, writhing in agony and whinging to the referee. But the biggest drama of all was Rooney's sending off in the 62nd minute for stamping on Carvalho's groin, the culmination, we are led to believe, of his frustration at being played as a lone striker!

So, with extra time not resulting in a clear winner we were into the 'dreaded' penalty shoot out. With Rooney off the pitch and back in the dressing room and Beckham nursing an injury, the queue for the spot was shortened. Lampard and Gerrard failed to convert their penalties. Carragher scored only to have his shot disallowed before fluffing his subsequent effort. The devil incarnate, since his perceived role in the Rooney sending off, Cristiano Ronaldo then stepped up and threw salt into England's wounds by scoring.

So, England finally improved with time but it was all too little, too late.

**England Squad**

*Manager: Sven Goran Eriksson*

| | Player | Appearances | Goals | Red | Yellow |
|---|---|---|---|---|---|
| 1 | Paul Robinson | 5 | 0 | 0 | 1 |
| 2 | Gary Neville | 2 | 0 | 0 | 0 |
| 3 | Ashley Cole | 5 | 0 | 0 | 0 |
| 4 | Steven Gerrard | 4+1 | 2 | 0 | 1 |
| 5 | Rio Ferdinand | 5 | 0 | 0 | 0 |
| 6 | John Terry | 5 | 0 | 0 | 2 |
| 7 | David Beckham | 5 | 1 | 0 | 0 |
| 8 | Frank Lampard | 5 | 0 | 0 | 1 |
| 9 | Wayne Rooney | 3+1 | 0 | 1 | 0 |
| 10 | Michael Owen | 3 | 0 | 0 | 0 |
| 11 | Joe Cole | 5+1 | 1 | 0 | 0 |
| 12 | Sol Campbell | 0 | 0 | 0 | 0 |
| 13 | David James | 0 | 0 | 0 | 0 |
| 14 | Wayne Bridge | 0 | 0 | 0 | 0 |
| 15 | Jamie Carragher | 2+2 | 0 | 0 | 1 |
| 16 | Owen Hargreaves | 3+1 | 0 | 0 | 2 |
| 17 | Jermaine Jenas | 0 | 0 | 0 | 0 |
| 18 | Michael Carrick | 1 | 0 | 0 | 0 |
| 19 | Aaron Lennon | 0+3 | 0 | 0 | 0 |
| 20 | Stewart Downing | 0+3 | 0 | 0 | 0 |
| 21 | Peter Crouch | 2+2 | 1 | 0 | 1 |
| 22 | Scott Carson | 0 | 0 | 0 | 0 |
| 23 | Theo Walcott | 0 | 0 | 0 | 0 |

Gary Neville: "We could not have given any more, but ultimately we lost and we are out of the tournament and going home on Sunday. For England and the expectations of the people, this is not good enough."

## Chapter 4:

# What went wrong?

**Date: 9th July 2006**
**By Harry Atchett, Sports Editor**
**The Daily Fail**

The World Cup 2006 is indeed over and the analysis of 'what went wrong' is well and truly underway. Whatever your day job - accountant, policeman, teacher, shop keeper, taxidermist, over the course of the World Cup competition it has become apparent that you, along with the rest of the nation, regardless of whether you support, watch or even like football, are actually something of an expert in this area. The jury is out but we all know exactly why England didn't cut the mustard or why England didn't make the grade.

But who's 'fault' is it, because, and trust us on this, as sure as eggs are eggs, someone is going to take the blame for England's 'failure' to bring the World Cup home to Blighty. Those who are actually paid to comment and pass judgment on the performance of our national side, or those in the know, fall into several camps when it comes to blame apportionment. The early names in the frames are Sven Goran Eriksson (nominated by young Michael Owen), Wayne Rooney (nominated by the howling masses), the wives and girlfriends or WAGS as they have become affectionately known (firm favourites with the press), and the weather (when all else fails...).

Someone, or something has certainly killed the national spirit and someone or something will have to pay. So, let us take a closer look at the line up in the dock, let's examine more closely the usual suspects, or, more specifically, the unusual suspects.

## Svendetta!

The easy target when the finger pointing starts has got to be the England manager, Sven. First and foremost he is a Johnny Foreigner who probably wanted Sweden to win all along. It's not entirely his fault that he was born non-British (parents have to shoulder some responsibility), but he has failed to redress this slight of fate by choosing to date an Italian and have a fling with a Swede rather than opt for one of our lovely English lasses. You've got to question his loyalty to the crown and the cross of St George.

But to bring the focus back to the footballing arena, it is generally agreed that, up until the decision to play a lone Wayne Rooney up front against Portugal and his small oversight of only selecting four strikers, two of whom had yet to be tested at this high level, Eriksson was considered a great strategist. Hardly any real surprise as the powers that be, those who select the England manager, oscillate between managers with passion but little in the way of planning or vision (Keegan, Taylor and their elk – sorry, ilk, we seem to be getting rather carried away with the whole Scandinavian thing) or those, like Sven, who are able tacticians but lack the fire (are we back to the snow and ice of the frozen north?) represented by the likes of Ron Greenwood.

Why, oh why, can't we find someone that embodies both technical ability and a passion that will raise and rouse the spirits of a nation? As far as emotional input goes, Sven's concession to the English public was to choose their 'big name' celebrity heroes (something you would never find Lippi doing). Interestingly enough, glancing through past manager profiles we notice that our greatest managers over the past sixty years – that is to say those whose win rate is in excess of 60%, are Sir Alf Ramsey (Feb '63 – May '74) and Glen Hoddle (June '96 – Feb '99). Sven falls just short of the mark at 59.7% as does Ron Greenwood (Aug '77 – July '82). By viewing the role call of England managers, we can clearly see that every fourth manager appointed to the role of England coach is (on paper at any rate) a gem. So, we need to jump three managers quick! Let's sack Steve McClaren with immediate effect (feel free to set up petitions calling for his removal), appoint two numpties and promptly show them the door taking comfort in the knowledge that whosoever is next drafted in will do us proud!

## Sweet F.A.

Being qualified executive coaches, and having been around a bit, we do know a thing or two about the subject of motivation. One of those little tips that you pick up along the way is that if you want to get the best out of people you don't sack them, demonstrating your complete lack of faith in their abilities and performance, only to set them a monumental challenge and expect them to pull out all the stops to ensure successes that will cover you in glory.

Of course there is always one individual who will seek to buck the trend by setting out to prove that you were wrong in your assessment (Klinsman falls nicely into this group on this world cup occasion) but in the main most folk balk at being judged and found wanting and will seek to find comfort and recognition for their attributes elsewhere. In light of the fact that the FA saw fit to give Sven his marching orders prior to this competition, is it any wonder that his formations were a little off from time to time? No, we believe it is hardly fair to lay the blame at Sven's door.

## It's only 12 yards

Let's turn our attention to the curse of the penalty shoot out. Speaking on the subject of penalties, Owen bemoans the fact that "we always seem to fall at that hurdle". Always? Actually no, not always.

The England fanzine site comes with a warning next to the heading of 'England Penalty Shoot Out Record' that reads "not pleasant reading". Indeed it isn't pleasant reading as the facts reveal that of the 7 world cup penalty shoot outs that England has been involved in they have been defeated on 6 occasions. But that isn't always, it's nearly always. Or to put it another way-sometimes we win penalty shoot outs!

Okay, these aren't the kind of odds to inspire anyone other than a Russian Roulette aficionado but they do provide a glimmer of hope, an opportunity for some positive thinking. Let's nip that in the bud. England is one of only two sides to have lost all three world cup penalty shoot outs that they have been involved in. There, told you, we're rubbish in this department. Funnily enough the other team who have lost all three penalty shoot outs they have been involved in are...Italy!

## Eleven good men and true

What of the players themselves? Let's start with the positive. Everyone loved Owen Hargreaves. Talk Back radio stations have campaigns to see him as the next England captain and, scour the web as we might we could find no negative comments, no digs at his abilities and no unsavoury characteristics or habits.

Lampard lacked imagination and Gerrard couldn't play with Lampard (you can almost picture young Steve's mother standing at her kitchen door, slippers on her feet, telling young Frank the sad news).

Rooney is an aggressive hot head who, although provoked to stamp on another player, felt remorseful enough to declare himself "gob-smacked".

Owen took the easy way out and had himself hospitalized before anyone could criticize his performance.

Joe Cole wasn't there when it counted and Beckham wasn't there where it counted and was self absorbed enough to forget to pass on any words of encouragement to Lennon for whom he was substituted.

To sum the players up, in the words of one of the Sugababes, whose incisive analysis cuts to the heart of the matter, "I don't think the team are playing at their best at the moment".

Having turned the floodlight on the manager, players and the fact that they have had to kick a ball into a net (however unreasonable this may seem) let's instead switch the focus to some external factors that may well have more of an influence than we may at first suspect.

## Football anthems

The purpose of these songs, beyond reaping a lorry load of cash for their creators, performers, producers, sound engineers, promoters, studio providers and stylists, is to rouse the nation to unify behind their national team.

'World in Motion' New Orders offering back in 1990 still sets feet a tapping and John Barnes rapping segment can easily be played over in the minds eye.

Oldies can still smile and wipe a tear from our eyes when 'Back home' (1970) faintly echoes, from a bygone age, in the overstocked warehouse of our memories.

Even the Baddiel and Skinner - 'Three Lions', with it's negative 'we're all doomed' lyrics inspires hope in the most ardent pessimist. Communication, as we all know, (or rather would know if communication were a lot better) is only 7% about the words with the remainder relying on body language and tone to convey the message. So, as long as we sing –

*"So many jokes, so many sneers*

*But all those oh-so-nears*

*Wear you down, through the years"*

– in a joyous, gutsy, upbeat manner whilst leaping energetically in the air, waving our scarves and whirring our rattles, we'll be OK. Forget the reality of results and performance, it would appear the success of a world cup tournament is perceived directly in relation to how good the world cup song is. No wonder we feel let down this year. Embrace's catchy little number – 'World at your feet' makes no mention of football whatsoever!

## Stars in their eyes

Looking even further afield for reasons (or excuses) for why it all went wrong, there is a possible, albeit tenuous link, between the makeup of a football team with regards to the star signs of it's squad and how they faired. A lack of sleep and way too much caffeine in the system lead to some quite startling revelations on the research front.

The German team are Scorpio heavy - reaching for the astrological forecast for the world cup period (thank you Shelley von Strunkel) we found that Scorpios were in for "complex situations... an unagreeable mood... with actions leading to complaints". We were obviously on to something.

We were shocked to find that England, like Brazil who were also sent packing at the quarter final stage, were Aquarius driven. There it was in black and white "when other people's decisions disrupt your life it is hard not to be annoyed". Too true! The advice was to try and adopt a positive attitude- well, never let it be said that the authors of this book don't listen to Zodiac advice.

France have a high number of Leos and the stars were very clear on their fate - "an important person who is relevant to success will be involved in a clash of personalities". Clash of heads more like.

So, to Italy. Amazingly Italy was the only squad where all signs were represented and evenly so. A clear indicator, if ever there was one, that all would be well for them.

## Stand by your man-icure

The WAGS, and their role, changed on a daily basis; they were seen as providing some light relief and entertainment in the England camp as well as being portrayed as a source of disruption and distraction at a time when focus was all important. How could the players possibly concentrate knowing that when they switched on the TV or opened a newspaper, one of their nearest and dearest would be dancing on a table, swigging Champagne from a bottle, staggering under the weight of designer shopping bags or jogging along in a 5 year old's gym kit! Steve McClaren plans to ban them from accompanying the team in future which seems a little harsh as what wife, girlfriend or mother would not wish to cheer her man on? Who will be there to accompany all the little Beckhams, Lampards and future Coles? The women folk at least provided some colour and interest to the proceedings. Are we to believe that our boys are so easily distracted?

Being English it is only right and proper that we end this chapter with a comment about the weather – it didn't help!

## Chapter 5:

# An imaginary call from the F.A.

*"I don't believe it!"*

We stopped talking mid-conversation and turned our attention to Jo who stood motionless, clutching the phone to her ear despite the fact that the dial tone was clearly audible and whomever she had been speaking with had gone.

*"What's happened?"*

*"Are you OK?"*

It was hard to work out whether the news she had received had been good or bad.

*"I can't believe it."*

*"Come on, tell us, what's going on?"*

The colour began to rise in her cheeks and the corners of her mouth began to betray the beginnings of a smile. The smile grew. The smile turned into a grin. The grin turned into laughter.

"You remember the other day when we were talking about the World Cup performance and how the England team could do with some serious coaching?"

Ged and Janice nodded, it had been a heated discussion following England's exit from the World Cup. Emotions had been running high and we had been appalled at the negativity and fatalism displayed by players, press and fans alike. We had even written on the back of a beer-mat (as anybody who knows anything about goal setting will appreciate you need to do) that our purpose was to help turn the team around before the next World Cup by raising awareness of the power of positive thought and self belief. Of course we remembered that conversation.

*"That was Brian Barwick of the F.A., the Chief Executive of the English Football Association."*

*"Yeah, right!"*

*"It really was."*

Jo is an honest sort. Honest as the day is long. If Jo says the F.A. was on the phone, mad as it may seem, you kind of have to believe her.

An awkward moment followed.

*"What did they want?"*

*"He's got a meeting with the board tomorrow afternoon and wants to put a proposal to them to adopt a coaching approach. He's asked for a 10 point action plan from us on how to turn the team's fortunes around. What do you reckon?"*

*"I'll get the paper, Janice, you get the pens."*

*"Someone grind the coffee beans, there's work to be done."*

# Memo

**To:** Brian Barwick, Chief Executive,
England Football Association

**From:** Janice Barnett, Ged Palmer, Jo Simpson; authors of 'They thought it was all over - they were right!'

**Subject:** How a change of mindset can empower the England Football Team to win the World Cup, South Africa 2010

**Date:** 15 July 2006

Further to our conversation earlier today, please find below 10 key areas, where we believe the application of our coaching techniques will make a real difference to the performance of the England football team and deliver outstanding success.

1. Vision and Goal Achievement: How to create a football vision for the England team and make the dream a reality
2. Know Your Values: How appreciating what matters most will drive the players and team to their ultimate achievement
3. A Reality Check on Beliefs: How to shake off limiting self talk and remove those beliefs that are holding England back
4. Getting the Balance Right: How to achieve the right balance between the demands of winning for club and country and other aspects of your life
5. Visualisation: How to imagine perfect performance and realise it on the pitch

6. Questions that Change Mindsets: How asking the right questions can challenge thinking and overcome limiting beliefs to move the team forward
7. Managing Change: How to develop an effective strategy for managing change to produce winning results
8. A Contract With the Fans: How, by building trust, developing mutual respect and sharing expectations, the fans can help create England's successful future
9. Motivational Environments: How to create an atmosphere that propels the team to exceptional performance time and time again
10. Celebrating Success: How to celebrate each step of success and gain momentum on the road to victory in South Africa 2010

We look forward to working with you and being part of the England Football team's very successful future.

Kind regards

Janice, Ged and Jo

'They thought it was all over - they were right!'

## Chapter 6:

# Our dream, our mission

As professional coaches, as well as avid England fans, we are eager to live our dream of coaching England to realise their true potential, culminating in winning the next World Cup in South Africa, by volunteering for the mission to coach the team.

Effective coaching starts with asking the right questions-

- What do England want to achieve as a team?
- What's currently holding them back?
- What would make the team a more cohesive unit?

We all have our own theories on these subjects but it is through encouraging the team to ask these, and many other questions, of themselves, that the best results will come.

Rather than telling the team what to do, the coaching way is to support, in this case the England team, to find solutions for themselves.

In the pages that follow we offer the England team coaching techniques that can be applied through 10 key areas that make for a successful winning team posing questions along the way that will challenge current thinking and open up new perspectives.

The effectiveness of a coaching approach is seen time and time again as individuals and groups achieve results they could previously only ever dream of. Creating a shift in the team's mindset combined with locking onto that special something will engage and inspire every member of the team. A greater commitment to change for the benefit of not only themselves but for the greater good of the whole team and, in this case, of the entire nation, will follow!

We do offer suggestions, advice and observations at certain points in our book based on our professional expertise as well as our research on World Cup winning teams. We have included tips and ideas as well as examples of practises and solutions that we believe will enhance results or are proven best practice. We hope such insights will add to our overall aim - to inform and stimulate our readers into considering how we can all play a part in this mission to transform our national football team into World Champions!

So, forward to South Africa 2010, let us consider first how a team can create its own vision and then set about making it a reality.

## Who am I to be Brilliant?

*"Our worst fear is not that we are inadequate; our deepest fear is that we are powerful beyond measure. It is our light, not our darkness that most frightens us. We ask ourselves, "Who am I to be brilliant, gorgeous, talented and fabulous?" Actually, who are you not to be? You are a child of God; your playing small doesn't serve the world. There is nothing enlightened about shrinking so that other people won't feel insecure around you. We were born to make manifest the glory of God within us. It is not just in some of us, it is in everyone; and as we let our own light shine we unconsciously give others the permission to do the same. As we are liberated from our own fear, our presence automatically liberates others."*

— Marianne Williamson quoted by Nelson Mandela

## Chapter 7:

# Vision and goal achievement

### Key Area 1: How to create a football vision for the England Team and make the dream a reality...

As any footballer and football fan knows, the goal is to progress by winning each game. While focusing on each match is important, it is neither a necessary nor sufficient condition of success in itself. For an individual or team to achieve truly amazing performances that lead to winning not only matches but tournaments and championships further foresight is required.

If you want to achieve outstanding results, in any walk of life, you need to have more than just goals. You need a 'vision' or 'dream', a clear picture of what you want to achieve that inspires action to create a reality; provides direction and meaning to your efforts and goals, and a compelling reason to succeed. And we're not just talking about the world-shaking dreams of Martin Luther King, Richard Branson or Nelson Mandela here.

Having a compelling personal vision which drives an individual so completely that they can and do achieve exceptional feats is something quite unique and, in our view is the common 'x factor' associated with outstanding performances in any field you care to mention.

In our research, we came across stories of individuals in all walks of life who realised their potential against all the odds, empowered by a personal vision of what they wanted to be, do or become.

In the sporting world, there are many examples of great sportsmen and women who realised a dream or followed their vision often overcoming 'impossible' odds and difficulties along the way and showing tremendous courage and determination. For instance, the legendary examples of Lance Armstrong, who overcame cancer, or Carl Lewis, an athlete from a poor black neighbourhood, Paula Radcliffe, a woman who had never run distance until her twenties and had been written off as too old and untrained, or (our personal favourite) Sir Bobby Moore – a working class East Ender and a school failure.

## So, where is the Vision in the England team?

This is not to suggest that individual players don't have a vision.

On the contrary, we applaud when we read of David Beckham, for example, who had a personal vision in his childhood of building a Soccer Academy to help children learn how to play football. He is achieving that vision through establishing The David Beckham Football Academy in both London and Los Angeles.

What we are asking is more specific:

Where is our England team's football vision? And how does that translate into a common vision to realise their potential in performances on the pitch?

For a team to become a highly successful, high-performance team, the members have to develop a shared vision for themselves, of what the team is there to accomplish, to contribute, to live (and die) for, to leave as its mark on history: a vision which reflects its members' values and beliefs and sustains and nurtures its goals, performance and achievements.

We're not just talking about the vision of a team to get through its next game: it's much more significant, long-term and far-reaching.

*"Some people believe football is a matter of life and death, I am very disappointed with that attitude. I can assure you it is much, much more important than that."*

— Bill Shankley, Liverpool FC

By developing and clarifying its vision, and only then setting out its goals to achieve that vision, a team will produce extraordinary - as opposed to just ordinary - results.

If team members all share a vision then their hearts and minds will focus on achieving that vision. That the ingredients to building such a common vision exist already, we have no doubt. A fine expression of an individual player's insight into part of what that vision might be is provided by the England mid-field player, Frank Lampard, who was interviewed prior to England's very first game in Germany 2006 (when confidence was high), against Paraguay, in which England dominated for the first 20 minutes before falling away dramatically:

*"The way to stamp our authority is to play our own game. Teams in the World Cup, especially South American teams, might find it hard to deal with an English-type game that we play better than anybody else-with a lot of pressure, playing to our attacking instincts and working hard- even if it means being a bit physical. That's the way we play."*

This is part of an individual's vision of the England football team, which says something about footballing values and beliefs, i.e. 'how we play, what is important to us, what distinguishes us from others, what is successful about us and what is our identity as a team'.

The question is: why can't such beliefs be used as the basis for the team to develop a common shared vision which defines their own standards of who they are, who they want to become and what their peak performance might look like?

We contrast Lampard's (in hindsight, wishful rather than realistic) views on how the team should play with David Beckham's reflections on England's performance after the slender win against Ecuador in their 3rd match:

*"It was an ugly performance but it is what we wanted and we will take ugly".*

Suddenly the confident, though incomplete, (Lampard) vision of a footballing style or brand value has been replaced by a rather more cynical 'win no matter-how ', summed up by Beckham's closing remarks which became the repetitive mantra of the team press conferences:

*"...we'll get better."*

The vision needs therefore to be more than one individual's view, it must reflect and bring together the whole team, and it should endure from one game to the next and be resilient to results, carrying the team forward in its chosen direction.

It must also appeal to the heart as well as to the head, saying as much about values, beliefs (which we examine in greater detail in later chapters) and ways of winning as tactics and formations.

A Vision must be inspirational, encourage passionate commitment and emotional bonding between the team members and also focus attention on evolution to a future desired state.

We would add that it needs to be easy to understand - defined and understood in the team's own language – too complex and you might as well not have one at all!

Part of Italy's head coach Marcello Lippi's vision expresses itself in terms of the team's identity – 'we are who we are, we know who we are'. The following was said by him shortly before the World Cup Final in Berlin:

*"This is the realisation of a dream that has lasted a very long time. We know anything can happen, but we will show all our strengths, our great enthusiasm and see what happens in the final"*

He goes on to reveal in the same interview the leader's role to share and inspire the rest of the team to a common motivating vision, to live and breathe the dream, although there are only a few tantalising glimpses of the details of that vision towards the end of the interview:

*"I have always considered being leader of this national team to be something magical. From the first day I started up to now, that feeling hasn't changed. For the past two years, I have tried to transmit this feeling to all my players and they have responded with their great enthusiasm, which has also helped me....Italian football is great football. It is very playful football."*

Lippi praised his players for the way they had overcome every obstacle, including the match fixing scandals back home, to reach a final many thought was beyond them.

*"It's a great satisfaction-these lads are fantastic. I told them they should be proud of themselves for reawakening the enthusiasm and love for our country"*.

Without a shared vision, a team lacks propulsion, it loses direction, heart and soul, and when the going gets tough the team begins to fall apart or shut down as a unit, even though individual members may have their own visions on what the team is about.

It is important to include the whole team in shaping the vision and engage the mind of each and every team player on how they can contribute to the greater good of the whole team.

But how can this be done?

We suggest coaching the England team through the following as the first steps in creating the vision:

## Building a common Vision

How far is the England Football Team going in the next World Cup?

What is important in that journey?

What do we, the England Football Team, want our fans to say about us?

What will make us proud to be an England football player?

What will make our fans proud to be our fans?

What will our legacy be for English football?

What will people say about us when they look back in 10, 20, 50 years time?

What will we tell our grandchildren about the England team we played in?

How will we move the game forward reflecting our values and beliefs about the game?

How can we give something back to our fans and the world through football?

## It wouldn't work here...

Heady stuff, I hear you say, not the sort of thing the pork-pie and Bovril brigade believe should be going on in the dressing-room of Accrington Stanley at half-time. But that is our point. Most football clubs play week-in-week-out, year-in-year-out, with little or no compelling vision of themselves, institutionalised through habit and custom and a limiting belief that success is just to survive in their individual league and maybe get a good run in the Cup.

The exceptions to the rule stand out alarmingly and prove our point: Watford and Wigan Football Clubs achieved incredible feats of league-hopping based on a long-term and commanding vision of success forged within their locker-rooms and promoted within their fan communities.

The England team is quite a different prospect from the lower league teams: a squad of the country's finest players drawn from the most successful teams in the land (and the world), on free transfers, that comes together for major tournaments and campaigns. Such a group, to be successful, has to operate beyond a narrow vision of just 'winning the next game' or 'getting through the group stage'.

Players, coach and team are selected not just 'to play for England' but 'to win for England' that is to develop, promote and act out an inspiring vision of a successful future which motivates and engages all of us to believe 'we can go all the way'. Creating a shared and inspiring vision in the England team is the foundation to creating a successful and winning mentality and a common purpose, of which we will have more to say later.

## Reinforcing the Vision

There are a number of techniques that can be used to reinforce a team's vision once it has been created and developed by the players.

An example of one method of reinforcement is for a team to create a Vision Board filled with images and symbols of success as they have defined it, and which acts as a continual reminder and nurturer of their dream. Such symbols might include a picture of the FIFA World Cup placed alongside a photo of the Soccer City Stadium in Johannesburg, South Africa, with a picture of the England Squad, a diagram of a tactical formation the team is mastering and images of successful penalties (these are just examples and are not intended to be prescriptive). Displaying the Vision Board in a prominent place at the team's base maintains focus and concentrates thoughts, energy and mental power on success and the road ahead.

For those who are inspired visually, a Vision Board can be a useful stimulus. Other stimuli can be employed to appeal to other senses. For example, recordings of inspirational team talks by the coach or captain will stimulate auditory senses. A piece of music, even an anthem that the team has chosen to associate with their vision creating a certain mood, can be used to tap into emotions.

Other reinforcement techniques include quiet reflection time as part of the training schedule or as part of a team briefing in which the team focuses for a few minutes on an aspect of their vision. Teams can also choose to review and challenge themselves with the vision questions earlier in this chapter and which were used to initially create the team vision.

Unconventional as some of these methods may seem, they can have a powerful effect on the team's vision, strengthening and sustaining the dream especially during times when the team has not met up for a while and has lost some focus.

*"Vision without action is a daydream. Action without vision is a nightmare"*

— Japanese proverb

## Goal Achievement: How to Achieve the Vision

So far we have looked at the importance of defining a vision for the England team. To convert that vision into reality requires setting and achieving goals through the activities we call the 5 P's:

**Planning & Preparation:** defining and setting a plan of goals and objectives that connect with the vision

**Practice and Performance:** building the skills, competencies and capabilities to achieve the plan and then putting them into practice

**Performance Review:** examining results and comparing these against planned objectives, identifying successes as well as areas for improvement

## Planning & Preparation

Goal-setting and goal reviewing may seem the stuff of board-rooms rather than the locker room, but consider these comments on England's 2006 performance in Germany by Sir Clive Woodward who led England to victory in the 2003 Rugby World Cup in Australia.

*"Look at every single thing that went wrong,"* said Woodward, listing poor penalty kicks, Wayne Rooney's red card in the quarterfinal, under-performing leading players and the inclusion in the squad of untested teenager Theo Walcott. *"Each was caused by a fundamental lack of preparation."*

After defining and focusing on the team's vision, the Coach and players then need to set their goals of how they will achieve the team vision, to be the best they can be. An example of a long-term goal would be 'Winning the World Cup in 2010' but such a goal has to connect with the vision, values and beliefs system (covered in later chapters) of the team, i.e. the meaning of the term 'winning' needs to be explored and defined in terms that all Team members can relate to as part of the Vision.

To make long-term goals more manageable, the team then needs to break them down, setting goals to achieve in the medium and short term. A challenging goal can be overwhelming or worse still, lead to complacency if it is not broken down into meaningful and smaller targets and plans that fire up motivation.

For example, an intermediate goal might be winning the next European Championships with defined targets for the team: tactical formations and flexibility, fitness levels, adaptability, etc.

Working back from the long-term goals, the team then needs to set goals for each year and have a strategy for quarterly goals to remain focused on what they want to achieve overall.

## When vision isn't enough

Without a focus on specific goals which lead to realising the vision, a team runs the risk of staying in la-la land, dreaming but not working towards results, 'all inspiration without perspiration'.

A nice example of this pitfall was afforded by the Brazilian team whose languid performances and ignominious exit in Germany 2006 was attributed to a complacency bordering on recklessness.

With the clock ticking down in Frankfurt, trailing 1-0 to the French and 20 minutes from elimination, it was revealing to observe how six of the Brazilian players continued to casually stroke the ball around in their own half with no sense of urgency to gain an equaliser.

As Cafu, the Brazilian Captain, ruefully admitted later while nursing their quarter-final defeat against France,

*"I had the sensation that we felt we could settle the game from one moment to the next".*

The Brazilians acted like favourites, but never played like favourites, lulled into a false sense of security and lack of focus on goal achievement by their pre-tournament billing as favourites. They sheltered in fantasy football but were disconnected from the reality of their own results on and off the pitch.

## Practice and Performance

It's critical that a Vision is followed up with actions that are planned and carried through. This will involve bringing the squad together to review team progress on their goals on a regular basis as well as individuals on their specific goals.

Goal-setting has implications for selection decisions on players. The Coach must consider how he can get the best out of the long-term investment in team development that focused planning and preparation involves. A settled and established squad of players is likely to be far more committed to focused goal setting and to their achievement over the long-term!

The value of planning and goal setting to produce memorable performances was no more apparent than in the German team who showed typical Teutonic efficiency in their build up to the tournament. Although a relatively young and inexperienced squad led by a Californian-based coach, Jurgen Klinsman, many were surprised by their adventurous and attacking style of play and self-belief, although given only an outside chance prior to the tournament. Success on the field was attributed to their meticulous preparations at coaching camp, in spite of a series of lack lustre results in the year prior to the tournament. The German midfielder, Torsten Frings, summed up their feelings of progress towards achieving planned goals:

*"We now have a lot of self-confidence. We are very fit and have shown this during the tournament so far... We worked very hard with the big target in mind .I think we have improved in all areas and it is showing."*

In order to continually re-assess what the team has already achieved and what still needs to happen, milestones need to be set that lead to a target date (four years, one year, six months, three months, monthly, weekly and even daily).

## Performance Review

A team journeying towards success must continually review its goals, comparing its achievements with its stated objectives and continually reminding and reinforcing the link to its larger vision.

Gianluigi Buffon, the Italian goalkeeper, commented on the importance of keeping the goal in sight with single-minded determination:

*"We are playing in the biggest competition in the world and the match-fixing scandal (involving prominent Serie A teams back home in Italy) has never once distracted us from our goal."*

Buffon was due to beat the all time clean –sheet record in the World Cup set by his compatriot Walter Zenga who went 517 minutes without being beaten at Italia '90.

*"Of course I am interested in beating the record, but only if it means Italy have not conceded a goal in the final", said Buffon. "I want to make my dream come true, win the game and finally touch the World Cup trophy".*

Another example of focusing on the team's goals was provided by Thierry Henry of the French team:

*"We were not listening to what people were saying. We were just concentrating on playing as a team. That is what the team is all about. We never cared about our critics-we just got it done."*

Unless the team members see the value of certain goals and how they contribute to the overall vision, belief in the goal will be weak and will undermine and even lead to goal-failure.

For example, the goal of playing in a certain tactical formation will not be achieved if it is not fully understood and believed in by all team members as a necessary step towards a dream of creating a team with tactical flexibility (if that is part of the team's vision).

All the planning and preparation in the world will be wasted, if it does not engage the team and is not practised with belief and intensity. Sven's comments on penalty drills at the morning press conference after the Gelsenkirchen defeat are apocryphal:

*"We practised penalties so much; I really don't know what more we could do about it. We have practised for the last four or five weeks. They have been very good in training but when it comes to the final stages we miss it."*

Did the team really believe in all that practice? How seriously did they take it? What goals and objectives around penalty taking under performance conditions were not covered?

## For goals to really engage the team they must be:

- Personal **"We will..."**
- Positive **"We can..."**
- Present Tense **"We are..."**
- Balanced – take into account all the key activities to succeed (practice, skill development, visualisation & mental conditioning, team and individual review meetings)
- Include 'hot' words, that is words which carry emotional power and meaning for the players.
- Be challenging and stretching – to improve confidence and the feeling of significant progress
- Clearly link with the end benefit rather than narrowly focus on the barriers to be overcome, i.e. look beyond the wall to the successful outcome.

Finally, it is essential to developing a sense of progress and achievement within the Team that as goals and milestones are achieved they are recognised and celebrated.

We deal with celebrating success in our final chapter.

*"To accomplish great things we must not only act, but also dream: not only plan but also believe"*

— Anatole France (1844-1924)

## Chapter 8:

# Know your values

### Key Area 2: How appreciating what matters most will drive the players and team to their ultimate achievement...

### What matters most!

In this chapter we will consider how values are the foundation to developing a team that has focus, passion and purpose to achieve it's vision and the important role that leadership plays in creating a strong team mission based on such values.

Our Values are our blueprints, our driving forces and personal motivators. If you asked a player what mattered most to him he may say family, house, money or – in David Beckham's case – nice cars. However, these are all material gains, which are representational of what an individual's true values may be: recognition, achievement, respect, security, love and independence are examples of the core values in this scenario.

Values are the foundation of a player's character and identity. They drive performance and lead players to express themselves in particular ways with a football.

Edgar Davids, the Dutch international player, illustrates the driving force of his values of courage, determination and making a difference in the following excerpt from his World Cup diary:

*"People that know me well know that the streets are my background in many ways. That's where I learned The Game, the hustle, the determination and above all the technique of survival. Many times I had to play against opponents many times older, bigger and heavier than me. Even though it was sometimes a really intimidating experience I never backed down. Ever. That's the basic rule of the streets. Show fear and you're toast.*

*"Since I was determined to become a professional football player I realized at an early age that no matter what the circumstances, intense heat, bitter cold and or mean opponents, I had to give it all I had to make a difference, to make a name. And so I did."*

There is a strong sense of identity here, and an insight into how a player's values are an integral part of his game.

It is vital that the head coach is aware of an individual player's Values as this will give powerful insights into how to get the best from them. Our most successful Premier League Club Managers understand this and will use these insights constantly, almost instinctively, to create leverage and motivation.

Another example from Davids' diary where he illustrates how important football is to him in serving the values of equality and self expression:

*"I feel blessed to be part of one of the most beautiful inventions known to mankind: Football.*

*"I can hardly think of a more universal way of expressing yourself than playing around with a football, one on one, two on two or an all out game. It doesn't matter. The spirit stays the same. There is not one place on earth where people of all creed, colour and age fail to enjoy the magic of the football game."*

Questions that an England head coach may pose in selecting his squad for the World Cup:

- How genuine is the player's need for achievement (to take one value), when they already have achievement in spades through playing for their club sides?
- What will the World Cup bring them that they don't already have?
- What is it that their club manager knows about this player's values that can be used to get the best out of this player?

## Team Values

It is not enough to just understand individual values. Any team worth its salt has a clear set of team values. At national and club level, these values may include loyalty, achievement, recognition, contribution, pride, discipline and self-respect.

Like individual values, it is team values, which fire up performance and give identity and 'character' to a team and can be used to create a sense of mission or common purpose. Consider the following diary entry by Gian Luigi Buffon, the Italian goal-keeper, written back at the hotel prior to the final in Berlin:

*"Our group has demonstrated that we have what it takes to make it right to the very end, despite the criticism we've received. But right now, I'm too happy to worry about that because it would just make me angry. Call me old-fashioned, but when I heard the Italian national anthem playing before the match against Ghana I couldn't help feeling emotional. That's why I just can't understand how some people, like the comedian Beppe Grillo, can consider proposing supporting the teams that we play against, even as a joke. The people's enthusiasm, celebrating our wins in the streets, is the most beautiful thing in the world. All those fans singing made my hair stand on end and certainly got me over all the nerves I'd been feeling before our first match."*

Claude Makalele of France, one of the French veterans in the side who shared a strong value of contribution and sense of legacy reflected that:

*"Players such as me, Zidaine, Thuram and Barthez have gone out of our way to help the newcomers to adjust to the unique World Cup atmosphere.*

*"We believe we have a responsibility to pass on the baton to the new generation of international players after we have left the arena. It is important not just to do well in this tournament but to make sure the future of French football is in safe hands".*

If we look at the winning teams in World Cup Germany 2006, one thing that stands out significantly is a strong sense of common purpose based on shared team values which acted as a powerful emotional bond between players.

Gianluigi again expressed his feelings eloquently in the following extract from his World Cup Diary:

*"I've heard and read quite a few comments out there saying that we're not playing well. Well, we may not be the best at putting on a show, but that's just the way we are. We get stuck into to the heat of battle and what the fans want to see is their team fighting, suffering and making sacrifices in order to win. Basically, it's hard to just have fun at a World Cup because the pressure is just so great — you need to keep your feet firmly on the ground.*

*"Italy tends to show the best of itself when things get tough and some of the incidents that have happened have helped us to become even more tight-knit as a group."*

In the case of Italy, players described the 'anger' they all felt at the Italian team's abysmal performances and early exits in Japan/ Korea 2002 and Euro 2004. In addition, the Serie A match-fixing scandals back home in Italy contributed to their sense of injustice and frustration. The team's values of self-respect, recognition, commitment and achievement were called into question by the Italian media and led to a genuine shared emotional reaction which drew the team together. They used their anger as a spur to a common purpose of proving all their critics and doubters wrong through their results in Germany.

In the French camp, there was a similar unity of purpose to answer their critics, arising in their case from a national perception in France that the team couldn't score goals and was too old! Claude Makalele, the French central defender and veteran, captured this mood in his World Cup diary as the results started to prove their critics wrong:

*"Those who didn't believe in us must be feeling a little embarrassed now but we will not gloat. We will just keep our minds on what lies ahead."*

On 7th July, you can feel Makalele's satisfaction when what had at first been scathing derision by the fans had turned into a rallying cry for the whole nation which reflected the French team's values of recognition and respect:

*"There is a new chant among the France fans at the World Cup finals. It has changed from "Allez Les Bleus" to "Allez Les Vieux" (The Old Men).*

*"I am told it is also a popular chant back home in France where 300,000 people gathered in the Champs Elysees after the win against Portugal on Wednesday.*

*"t was an emotional moment especially for myself and the other "old men" in the squad. Players like myself Lillian Thuram, Fabien Barthez and, of course, the Grand Master Zinedine Zidane.*

*"We all had the same feelings before the World Cup began. We were growing old but we all felt we had one last chance for glory with the national team. Now we are 90 minutes away from living our dreams."*

The team is much more than the sum of its parts. If team values are to support the vision and the goals that England want to achieve, the team needs to establish what matters to them and what forms the basis of their dream.

Personal values will drive team performance if they are in harmony with the team values and overall team vision.

The first step is to decide which values are required for the team.

Questions that could be asked include:

- What is driving the team to win the World Cup?
- What is of utmost importance to the players as a team?
- What does playing as part of the current England team give the players?
- Which values need to be displayed for the players to optimise the team's performance?
- Which values need to be adopted to create a strong positive winning team?

Once the team values and vision have been set, the team players will know exactly what is expected of them and can integrate their personal values accordingly. If an area of values conflict occurs, differences need to be acknowledged and worked around. The key here is having an awareness of each other's values.

## Where was the passion?

Cynics may argue that some of our England players, fabulously wealthy and established stars in their own right, have individual purposes, motives and values which receive far greater attention than the more traditional demands of team work and collective effort. In an age dominated by commercial sponsorship, image management consultants, players' agents and ghost-biographers of 20 year-old 'legends', there may be some truth in that claim.

*"The problem I see is the rising tide of overblown egos infiltrating the team. They're more in love with themselves and their appearances than they are with winning for England. To them its self 1st, club 2nd and nation 3rd."*

—Yahoo England Fan Blog, dated 8th September, 2005, by drj3671

Whatever the reasons, in some England player interviews in Germany 2006, we detected a lack of shared team values and a corresponding weakness of purpose. Was this the root cause of the lack lustre England performances on the pitch, performances which were all the more perplexing in that they were by the same players who, for their club sides, excel week in week out?

Such hopeful statements from the players and the head coach as, the team "would gel" or "get better in time", "hopefully when we play a quality team", or "we've got the individual players to do it - to go all the way", suggest assumptions based more on hope and individual talent rather than confident and common team values.

A sense of complacency that the team would somehow spontaneously emerge as a fully formed high performance and purposeful unit as a result of time and luck (Sven's continual "we'll get betters") was initially present. The brittle confidence of such early statements was to degenerate into the "we'll take ugly" after the Ecuador game and finally the tearful post-Portugal "we were just not good enough".

As the former England Manager and inspirational football champion, the late Sir Bobby Robson observed after the tournament in a radio interview: *"Where was the passion? ... where was the hunger?"*

## Where indeed?

Looking at the dynamics involved in the formation of the England team in the run up to the World Cup 2006, there are lots of clues:

- Players with individual ideas, visions, dreams, goals and personal values, which weren't aligned with those of the team.
- Players who fulfilled their roles as captain at their existing clubs now came together to play for England as just another member of the team.
- A head coach who was 'sacked?' prior to the biggest, most prestigious event in football, affecting team morale, confidence, motivation and ability to work together.
- Constant changes of tactical formations both in the lead up to and during the tournament preventing the opportunity for the team to gel and create the team spirit required.
- The Rooney effect – will he / won't he be fit? So much pressure and hope placed on one individual!

Throw all these ingredients into the melting pot and what have you got?

### *A crisis of confidence!*

A team that lacks confidence is a team without a cause, a team without a common set of values or mission. In fact, we would go so far to say, it is not a team at all!

Most of the 2006 England World Cup Squad were already celebrities in their own right prior to the tournament, whereas, by comparison, the winning team of 1966 was a different story – this team was driven by raw emotion, not money or becoming famous. There was a hunger to succeed fuelled by the prospect of performing in front of the home supporters. Most were unknown until they became heroes as a result of this magnificent victory and are still well known today owing to this one event alone. There were no sponsorship deals or focus on becoming celebrities.

*What might the team of 1966's values have been?*

*Passion, respect, trust, pride, contribution maybe?*

Yes we realise times have moved on, yet fundamentally when you look at what drives a teams' behaviour, surely there are lessons to be learned here or a winning formula to be discovered.

## Leadership

No discussion of team values and common purpose can ignore the role of leadership as a catalyst for their development.

What should we look for in a good leader?

A team leader needs to be an extraordinary person, who embodies the team's values and at the same time supports, encourages, motivates and fires up individuals within the team to action.

Someone who is able to see the big picture and yet not lose sight of the details: to honour and recognise skills in others and to continually expect more from them.

A leader needs to influence their team to continually raise the bar, break out of their comfort zone and commit to achieving higher standards. A true leader is a realist, is truthful and honest in their opinions and concerns whilst recognising their own limitations.

Phew! Quite a list!

A widely admired and exceptionally successful leader is Sir Alex Ferguson of Manchester United. Here's an interesting example from Lee Sharp's (ex. Manchester United player) World Cup blog on how Sir Alex creates a sense of mission and team values at Old Trafford:

"When we were at Man Utd and winning everything, the mentality was us against the world. Alex Ferguson brought us all together as a little community. It wasn't just the 11 players that went on the pitch, it was the squad, the reserves, the apprentices, all the staff. It was like, "Everybody hates us, everybody wants us to lose, so let's shove it up them and go out there and beat everybody."

In this World Cup, Zinedine Zidane's leadership should be recognised, leaving aside an unfortunate altercation with Marco Materazzi in the Final, for his sense of mission, drive and commitment to serving his team.

Claude Makalele again:

*"I have noticed what an important part Zinedine Zidane plays when we are in the training camp. Everyone looks up to him because he has been such an outstanding player during his career.*

*"But he is a very humble and down-to-earth person who goes out of his way to integrate players like Chimbonda and Ribery into their new surroundings. There is a great team spirit developing and we cannot wait to get started.*

*"But you get the feeling now he is on a personal mission here in Germany to bow out on a real high – and there would be no better way than to do it by lifting the World Cup trophy."*

Another exceptional role model and a great football leader was Sir Bobby Moore and yes, we are referring to 1966 again, because we feel there is a lot to learn from the behaviours displayed then. During the last few seconds of extra time in the '66 World Cup final, when Bobby Moore had the ball on the edge of the England penalty area, totally focused, with clarity and purpose amidst the screams of Jack Charlton to kick the ball out of play, Bobby Moore calmly looked up and perfectly passed the ball for Geoff Hurst to complete his hat trick. By taking this choice, Moore showed vision, purpose and confidence in the team to win the game convincingly – a winning mentality that inspired all those around him.

Together with Alf Ramsey, he was part of a coach-captain partnership that produced a powerful and magnetic influence on the team and which was able to channel the team's raw hunger for success into positive results.

A critical leadership partnership in Germany 2006 which created a common unity of purpose, an "iron will to win" as one commentator called it was seen in the victorious Italian team. It was the ability of the head coach, Lippi and his captain, Cannavaro, to direct the "anger" in the team and create the leverage and purposeful aggression that drove the team on to far exceed their critics' expectations.

As we shall see in a later chapter, Lippi selected his players on their performances alone. Any sign that a player's commitment to the team's purpose was lacking, and they were dropped-regardless of their 'reputation'

## Formula for passion

So how can we create an England team fired with passion and commitment to succeed based on common values?

We suggest the England team needs to get back to basics and search its soul for the meaning and the values that will drive it towards its goals. A good starting point would be the 'place of pain', the experience of defeat and humiliation in the 2006 World Cup and 2008 Euro qualifying campaign.

*"All the players are still hurting from the World Cup and we've got to use that experience to drive us on in the future."*

— Steven Gerrard

The disappointment and universal sense of under-achievement should be a spur to get serious about what the team wants in setting its next goals for South Africa 2010.

- What questions could the team ask themselves? Maybe the following:
- What do we want to achieve in the next tournaments?
- How important are these goals to us?
- What do we have in common that really matters to us?
- What do we want to prove: to ourselves, to our fans, to our nation?
- What do we want to be recognised for that will be different to our current reputation?

What do we need to do differently to achieve success?

Setting GOALS based on team VALUES, gives the team passion and purpose. Add to the equation, a set of positive BELIEF statements and BEHAVIOURS as the driving force to this combination and the end result – A team with a winning mentality!

Sounds impractical or unlikely? Many organisations such as Apple and Disney, BP and Hewlett Packard are now creating powerful work teams based on this very process of identifying shared common values which are aligned with goals, beliefs and behaviours.

Value elicitation sessions with the team form a basis on which to set goals, create empowering beliefs and identify supporting behaviours.

This is best illustrated by the following example of creating a common value of self–control and discipline (Wayne Rooney, please pay attention!):

**Values:** Being a successful England team player, we value self-control and discipline

**Belief:** Teams who win games have all 11 players on the pitch after 90 minutes

**Goal:** Giving ourselves the best chance of winning every game

**Supporting behaviour:** We demonstrate these values by abiding by the rules of fair play, exercising self-control in tackles, our reactions to the referee's decisions, helping team members to avoid conflicts with the referee and through preventing and avoiding blatant fouls

Part of our Common Purpose: we want to be respected by our peers and fans as a team that sets and maintains a high standard of fair play, self control and self discipline whatever the opposition's tactics or provocation, however questionable the referee's decisions.

The above process is straightforward and can be followed for other, values, belief and goals alignments:

**Team Improvement**

What do we need to focus on to get the best improvements out of the team?

What behaviours will demonstrate our focus on improvement?

What do we need to do to answer our critics?

**Team Honesty:**

How honest are we are about our results/performances compared with the hype?

How honest are we with each other?

How will we know we are demonstrating our commitment to be open and honest?

**Team Contribution:**

Let's not rely on one individual – we are all an equal part of this team and everyone has a part to play in contributing to our success.

How can we ensure we all pull our weight and contribute?

How can we all play to our individual strengths, whilst ensuring good teamwork?

The above list of examples will give a flavour of how to use this process. More values can be reviewed in this way to build up a set of commitment statements, a mission that all team members sign up to and feel strongly about. It is what is valued by the team that matters most in this alignment exercise and will create the launch pad for a shared common purpose.

## An Unstoppable Combination

An England team with values, beliefs and goals in alignment will have a powerful unstoppable winning combination that will enable them to move forward with purpose and confidence.

*"The secret is to work less as individuals and more as a team. As a Coach I play not my eleven best, but my best eleven"*

— Vince Lombardi

# Chapter 9:

# How healthy is England's belief system?

## Key Area 3: How to shake off limiting self talk and remove those beliefs that are holding England back...

There is so much emphasis placed on the physical side of the teams' training – the tactics, the skills, the techniques and the strengths of each player that, to a large extent, the psychological side of the player's behaviour - their attitude, determination and focus, has been overlooked.

So let's have a look in more detail at the effects and importance of an individual's mindset to the game. To do this, we need to understand what we mean by Mindset. Mindset is very much a matter of what we believe, or rather choose to believe. For example, if someone believes they are a failure, having sought out and stored evidence of their failures, shortcomings or situations that did not go well for them, this is what they will portray to the world. On the other hand, someone only choosing to store positive facts and evidence, taking the best from every situation will view the world in a much more optimistic way and will display this accordingly in their attitude, behaviour and language. Our beliefs are based on the way we choose to filter information, regardless of facts or evidence to the contrary.

'The Belief System' works in much the same way as a filing cabinet. We retrieve information in exactly the same way that we stored it, even if it has been in there for years. If evidence has been stored to support a lack of ability, such as 'I can't get crosses into the near post accurately', this belief will persist regardless of any evidence to the contrary, unless it is re-examined.

We all have a belief system, which forms from a very early age and continues to form throughout our life. Within this all our experiences are filtered to provide evidence that back-up our beliefs. The important element here is that we can choose to change our beliefs and recondition our minds.

## Clear out the clutter

Lets take a Health Check on the England team's belief system and look at what may be in those filing cabinets, it's time to clear out any old unwanted limiting negative files and replace them with exciting empowering positive shiny new ones.

## Limiting Beliefs – We are what we believe!

Let's examine some evidence - The infamous penalty shoot-out curse!

What a great place to start. There are so many limiting beliefs in this area, that we could have written a book on these alone! The penalty curse, as it is now affectionately known throughout the UK is a fantastic example of how not only the players, but the nation as a whole are storing this great whopping 'limiting belief' and self-fulfilling prophecy.

They thought it was all over before they began to take the penalties! And yes, they were absolutely one hundred percent right. It was already a foregone conclusion that England never win a penalty shoot-out. Not only was it the players who believed this, the commentators, the fans, the opposition, in fact we will go so far as to say the rest of the world believed it too! We were watching the England v Portugal World Cup quarter final in a bar in Dubai with a broad representation of nationalities and cultures. We heard comments from the England Fans sounding out around the bar such as "oh no!" or words to that effect – "this is it – it's all over!", "We are doomed – it's the penalty curse!"

"This is it – we are doomed?" We asked ourselves bewilderedly? We had got through to a penalty shoot-out with 10 men – what a great achievement and now "this is it!!?"

The Syrian gentleman supporting Portugal standing in front of us, with whom we had been having some mild banter throughout the game, turned calmly to us and said. "This is it – you are out now"...and yes, you've guessed it – he was right too!!

The commentators stating that Portugal have never lost on penalties and making negative remarks about England never winning penalty shoot outs simply added to the gloom!

So how have the England team allowed their own belief systems to affect their performance?

The players appear to be storing negative evidence to support their beliefs regarding penalty shootouts, based on their experiences in previous tournaments – Japan 2002, Portugal 2004, and now Germany 2006. This is illustrated in the following example:

Michael Owen states in his online diary of Germany 2006:

*"The penalty shoot-out is truly nerve-wracking, you have got ten seconds to just block everything out and try to focus on scoring a goal. It is more nerve wracking than anything else in the game."*

He goes on to say that there is so much pressure; thinking about the fans; people at home; in pubs around the country and the other team players behind him.

Here we have a great example of a limiting belief, which also highlights the use and calibre of self-talk and language that is going on inside his mind.

If Michael Owen believes the penalty shoot-out is truly nerve wracking, guess what – he is right!

Owen also states you have to **try** to focus on scoring a goal – How about removing the word **try** - you either do or you don't. The Oxford dictionary definition of try is: "make an attempt or effort to do something", so let's instead 'focus on scoring a goal.'

(Apologies and thanks to Michael Owen - you have given us some great examples here).

We have observed a cascade effect of these limiting beliefs on fans, commentators and in general the whole nation.

Based on the evidence of previous performances to date, the team and nation have chosen to believe that England are abysmal at penalty shoot-outs, yet research shows that 60% of penalties taken by England in World Cup matches have been converted. Not as high as some granted (the average across the board is over 70%) but still, the likelihood is they will score. How about we choose to build on this more positive belief of achieving 60% success instead?

The media further embed the negative belief, we seem to enjoy making a national pastime of destroying our heroes.

What are we doing as a nation to encourage our team and change the negative conditioning?

Our conversion rate of 60% is a fact but we can choose to store this data in a positive way through reframing or repackaging it. Let us instead present it as having a greater than 50 % chance of scoring.

How about we all choose to change our belief system, self-talk and use of language to support, empower and encourage our national team and begin to say such things as:

- What can we do to improve our 60% success rate when taking penalties?
- England are great when they truly focus on aiming the ball into the net
- We didn't win the last penalty shoot-out, how can we approach this differently next time?
- What do we need to believe about ourselves and our abilities and what do we need to focus on?
- We are learning what we need to do differently next time
- We can consider that every penalty shoot out is a fresh event, so statistically, before the first ball is struck, we have the potential of a 100% success rate

## How others have succeeded

Some examples of belief statements that led to victory can be seen through comments made by Sir Alf Ramsey during the 1966 World Cup Tournament.

*"Never change a winning team."*

This belief secured the 1966 winning world cup team. Alf Ramsey's belief was so strong that his decision to continue to play Geoff Hurst well and truly paid off, even though many were shocked that Jimmy Greaves now recovered from injury was not chosen.

*"Our best football will come against the right type of opposition - a team who come to play football, and not act as animals."*

This was Ramsey's indignant belief after England beat Argentina 1-0 in a bruising quarter final in the 1966 World Cup. And sure enough, when faced with Portugal in the semi-finals (yes – Portugal – the evidence is there that England can beat them!) and Germany in the Final, pure skilful Football was displayed and victory was had by a team the nation is still proud of today.

*"You've won it once. Now you'll have to go out there and win it again."*

Ramsey made the above statement during his brief team talk prior to the extra-time period in the 1966 final. Here he embeds the belief that England were winning against Germany with only 12 minutes to go until Germany equalized and forced the game into extra time. He demonstrates positive evidence for the players to focus on and win the match again, they did!

## All Change

It is now time for the England team to leave the past behind and move forwards with passion, intent, self-belief and confidence and win everything they put their mind to winning. This goes for the nation as a whole. Let's be proud of who we are, change those negative beliefs and support our national heroes publicly.

## 4 steps to change

### 1. Disassociate from Limiting Beliefs and negative evidence

Often it is the players who prevent themselves from achieving their full potential. They don't believe fully in themselves that they can do whatever it is they want to do. It is great for the team to learn from what went wrong in the past, but then to move on quickly. In order to change a limiting belief into a positive, more empowering one, the evidence stored needs to be changed.

Gary Neville is quoted as saying:

*"It will be a difficult couple of days. It's difficult now and it will be difficult tomorrow."*

If he believes it will be difficult, then it will be. An alternative more empowering statement could be to say:

We are an amazingly skilful football team, who overcome challenges effortlessly and easily.

It is pleasing to see that David Beckham was one step ahead with his thinking here in the following quote:

*"That was in the past - we're in the future now."*

**2. Create an Empowering Alternative Belief**

Firstly, you really have to want to change your thinking, performance or whatever it is that is holding you back. Find leverage (what is it that will really influence you to change?), get hungry and make the choice to take action. Look for the positive evidence in a situation and build on this.

An example of this would be our favourite – The Penalty shoot-out

Instead of, "oh no – not penalties"! or "That's it – it's all over now", more empowering beliefs could be:

"Great, an opportunity to get five bonus shots and score 5 phenomenal goals", or "What a great chance we have to demonstrate our skilfulness and excellence at how we score from the penalty spot".

**3. Positive Self-Talk and Belief**

The next step is to address the language we use both externally and internally. The words that we use are so powerful in building our confidence and self belief. This is not only the words that we say out loud, but also that little inner voice, affectionately known as the 'gremlin' that pops into our head in an attempt to hold us back. The gremlin needs to be replaced with positive empowering talk that will serve us in whatever we are doing. We examined some video footage of the press conferences held prior to the England v Portugal World cup game and we lost count of the amount of times the players used the words 'try' and 'hopefully'.

Peter Crouch: "There's a void to be filled and hopefully I can fill it. I think myself and Wayne can hopefully complement each other".

Steve Gerrard on Wayne Rooney: "Hopefully he could be our key man; I know he's still hurting from Portugal 2004".

Alternative more positive language could be:

- We are confident in our ability and certain that we will win
- We have great confidence in our technique
- We are a team of skilful players

Gary Neville highlights a great example of positive self-talk in his interview by saying, "What an opportunity? We can do something very good". Here we can leave the 'gremlin', grumbling because he's out of work.

### 4. Affirmations

Affirmations are an effective way to condition new positive thinking. These are positive statements that the players, team, and the fans can use to stack up positive beliefs in the unconscious mind to replace the negative beliefs that are currently residing there. Repetition is the mother of skill. Affirmations need to be repeated over and over again until they are conditioned in the mind and we begin to act as if they were already true. Through constant use and repetition, the new thinking becomes automatic.

A few examples are:

- We always score from the penalty spot
- We are the world's greatest penalty takers
- We embrace the opportunity to score from the penalty spot.
- We are the winning team
- We are proud to be English supporters

## Realise full potential

Research has shown that on average, human beings only operate at 40% of their true potential, imagine what could happen if we break down those barriers, remove the limiting beliefs, believe in ourselves and smash into that other 60%. Wow, we can see it now...England, The world's greatest football team are the new holders of the FIFA World Cup trophy and World Cup Winners, 2010

*"Whether we believe we can or we can't we are absolutely right"*

— Henry Ford

# Chapter 10:

# Balance

## Key Area 4: How to achieve the right balance between the demands of winning for club and country and other aspects of your life...

### Tipping the Scales

We read articles and watch programmes that tell us that in order to avoid stress we need a healthy balance in our lives. But how do we know whether our lives are balanced or not? What do we have to do to maintain this balance once we've found it? We can start by looking at the composition of our hours, days and weeks - 20% sleep, 60% work, 2% playing with the kids, 5% hobbies. We can also examine those aspects of our lives that overarch each of these areas such as our health, our financial situation or the amount of fun we are having. If you are perfectly happy with the split, chances are you will be feeling fine and life will be hunky dory. If, however, one area of life is receiving attention to the detriment of others you need to pay some serious attention to getting your balance back on track.

Let's take a closer look at this in the footballing context. We would all probably agree that a player's physical health, fitness and strength as well as their well being (looking after themselves; good diet; exercise; the right amount of sleep etc) are of paramount importance in securing their place in the England squad. Balance in a player's life, whether on or off the pitch, goes beyond these areas and is a contributing factor that influences a player's mindset and ultimately their performance.

Footballers performing at top international level do not have conventional weeks. For starters, they have a closed season and a league season. If their team has a successful run in domestic competitions additional matches will start to be added to their programme. If their team does well in Europe, more time for further games, travel and training, as well as energy will need to be found. This time and energy expenditure will encroach on other areas of a player's life and undoubtedly something else will have to give. If selected for the national squad, the scales are tipped even more heavily towards football commitment and away from relaxation, family and other activities.

*"It was important to have a break between the end of the domestic season and joining up with the national team squad - psychologically as much as anything else. You need to be able to take the pressure off and change your mindset a bit. Being with the national team is different to being with your club; you have to spend two and half months living together and sharing every minute with each other, so it is a different kind of challenge and before that, it is vital you have a break to relax and clear your head."*

— Xabi Alonso, Spanish midfielder, World Cup Diary

## What choices do they have?

Undoubtedly, footballers want to perform at their best and to do this they need to be in peak condition. However, from time to time an imbalance may occur when a new priority is forced upon them or a conflict of interest arises.

The important thing to remember is that in the majority of cases there is a choice – The choice to say YES or NO to activities or events that may impact their life balance. Whilst we are not suggesting for one minute, that the team say no to playing for their club and country and the extra matches this may entail, they may however need to pay closer attention to other aspects of their lives that can affect their equilibrium. Players need to understand that if they take on more than they are capable of dealing with, they could over burden themselves at the expense of some other commitment. What else are the players saying YES to, that can lead to consequences resulting in an imbalance in their lives?

One of the considerations to be made when asked to do the next sponsorship deal is whether saying YES to Armani sunglasses and publicity in the celebrity magazines means ultimately saying NO to privacy or time with their family.

Many factors have the potential to tip the balance which can subsequently impact performance on the pitch. Let's take Wayne Rooney as an example here. There was an enormous amount of pressure placed on him as the talisman for the team – a national press campaign of will he / won't he be fit to play; pressure from Sven to play and from Alex Ferguson to rest. How may this have affected Rooney – loyalty to England versus loyalty to his own club? By saying YES to playing was he saying NO to his health and fitness? With this pressure, in addition to that of playing the lone striker role is it any wonder 'Boy Wonder' was feeling internal conflict. A lack of balance that manifested in his aggressive behaviour ultimately resulting in Rooney venting his anger against Carvalho and being sent off in the match against Portugal.

## What is ideal balance?

Most of us are able to make a clear distinction between self-time and the usual daily demands placed upon us. Footballers do not always have this luxury. If a footballer wishes to grab a little private time to go to the pub, play a round of golf or go shopping in Sainsbury's, normal things that most of us take for granted, they may find themselves set upon by celebrity spotters or snapped by the paparazzi. Living with their personal and professional lives under constant scrutiny from the media, fans and general public provides additional challenges for the players to overcome. As a player becomes more successful, the potential to become a victim of that success increases. The player is transformed in effect from a private individual to public property. Whilst some players are happy to live in the glare of the publicity and actively court it, others find it an unwelcome side effect of stardom.

Let us take for example David Beckham. Together with wife Victoria, brand Beckham is now a worldwide phenomenon. His personal presentation skills have been honed and his entourage ensure that he is styled to perfection in whatever situation he may find himself. Glamorous, highly publicised, extravagant parties are held at his 'Beckingham Palace' residence in Hertfordshire and he appears on more magazine covers than most.

By contrast, Michael Owen is a little overwhelmed by the attention he receives. All he ever wanted, he tells us in his on line diary, was to play football although he accepts that the price to be paid for his success is an increased interest in all aspects of his life from press and public. He also, no-doubt, enjoys the many material things and opportunities that his celebrity have brought. 'Normality' in his life is a rare treat - finding space for it requires real effort.

The 'ideal' balance will be different for each individual player, it is an intensely personal thing – there is no set formula and it depends on what is most important to them at any given time. It is only when the balance in your life becomes adversely affected that stress may occur. Failure to address stress, whether through professional means or by making time to remove the causes of stress yourself, will, more often than not lead to serious consequences including mental or physical breakdown.

## Regaining Balance

It is to be expected that from time to time a player's life will feel out of balance – life happens! What is important is being able to identify when this occurs and knowing what is needed to bring the balance back. Ideally, prevention is better than cure and focus should be placed on having a healthy life balance. Recognising the triggers that could potentially put you out of balance and having a release means that you are able to take action in a pro-active manner and regain balance, before the scales begin to tip. Whilst you may not believe you have the time for a hobby or an activity that calms you and helps regain balance, such an investment could ensure you return to other activities refreshed and better focused.

Let's have a look at 'The effect of the WAGS'. If part of your healthy balance is spending time with your loved one, not seeing them can have a negative impact. Conversely if during competitions you prefer to focus solely on the sport, having your focus interrupted by reports of your partner's antics can be distracting and throw your balance out.

*"I have noticed in some reports that the England players have been allowed to spend some time with their wives and girlfriends in between matches. The French squad have never done that because it is considered too much of a distraction."*

— Makalele

Being residents of Dubai, we can't help but notice that one of the ways players like to restore balance is to retreat here for relaxation and privacy. With the majority of the team having purchased homes here, we will be hoping for invites to the house warming parties soon (which incidentally is another great way, we would recommend for them to achieve balance).

## Maintenance Programme

Our top 5 tips for the England Player's to maintain an ideal balance on a daily basis are:

1. **Know your individual values and honour them on a daily basis**

   If 'Freedom' is an important value, ensure that achieving this is part of your lifestyle to avoid stress.

2. **Check your thinking and self talk**

   What messages are you giving yourself? Ensure your beliefs are empowering ones that will move you forward rather than limiting ones that will hold you back.

3. **Well-Being**

   In order to be in balance, it is vital to look after your well-being, not only when building up to a match, but constantly to ensure optimum energy is always available to tackle anything that comes your way. This includes the fuel you put into your body, the right amount of sleep and regular exercise. As they say 'You are what you eat'

4. **Consider the consequences of YES v NO**

   When asked to do the next sponsorship deal – What will the impact of saying YES really mean? How will the scales be tipped and what will have to give in your life to accommodate the deal. Or, on the flip side, what is the Impact of saying NO? The England team said NO to meeting fans at Stansted airport, which then meant they were saying YES to bad publicity. The key here is choice and awareness of the impact it has.

5. **Know your own balance**

   Be aware of the triggers that could potentially put your life out of balance and those that are required to restore balance. If you know that being away from your family for more than a week causes you distress ensure that some private quality time is planned when you are reunited. If you know that missing your regular round of golf for more than two weeks in a row causes restlessness plan your priorities in advance. The key here is being aware of timings and triggers that work for you personally.

There is no doubt about it, being under the spotlight for every move they make will affect the England teams' life balance. Awareness of the potential causes of imbalance and ways to address these, allows you to plan accordingly and achieve stability leading to a healthy balance in your life.

*"Life is what happens while you are busy making other plans"*

— John Lennon

# Chapter 11: Visualisation

## Key Area 5: How to imagine perfect performance and realise it on the pitch...

One of the most powerful coaching techniques used in modern sports is visualisation.

Visualisation is the technique of practising or rehearsing a physical movement, action or manoeuvre by imagining it being performed to a perfect level or standard of competency 'in the mind's eye'.

Since the mid 1980's when it was first advocated as a coaching technique for Tennis players ('The Inner Game of Tennis' by Tim Gallwey, 1986), visualisation has become a respectable and accepted practice in many sports.

Golf coaches, for example, are to be seen up and down the fairways of the world, taking their clients patiently through visualisations of strokes and shots, before letting them loose.

Nowadays, visualisation is an essential part of any sports coaching curriculum and every year sees waves of new sports coaches arrive in the sports community with these proven techniques.

## How does visualisation work?

- Visualisation uses the same parts of the brain as when the body is physically performing the sports activity. Your brain and neural pathways get to practice telling your arms and legs how to move without them having to actually move.
- It is sometimes falsely assumed that vision is the only sense involved in visualisations but in fact, hearing, smell, touch and even feelings or emotions are also important.
- The more detailed your visualisations are, the more effective they may be in helping you improve your game. This includes, for example, how the field smells or how the arena sounds. The closer a visualisation is to operant conditions, the more effective learning and the resultant performance will be.
- It is recommended to keep visualisations as specific and detail-oriented as you can. The coach or trainer can help to break things down so the sportsman or woman really understands how he or she should be moving.
- The best visualisations are those that happen in real time. Mentally the player goes through each action, step-by-step just as they would in practice.
- Since it can be mentally tiring to really focus on visualisations, it is also advisable to start out slowly. Eventually, it becomes easier to keep visualising for longer and longer stretches of time. There is a definite practise effect and visualisation can, ultimately, become a highly developed skill.
- Visualisations have been used primarily for correcting or re-aligning particular mechanical-motor skills. For example, modelling the correct body alignment before getting the player to focus on the move and on doing it perfectly over and over until the move becomes automatic in the brain and requires less attention in performance.

- It is a myth that visualisation only works if applied within 24 hours of performance. Visualisation is an effective tool even if you're laid up with a sports injury. If you're too hurt to practise, you can at least picture yourself going through the motions. It can even speed your recovery.

So far, so good. Nothing new here you might be saying. After all, we all know that many of our English footballers practise hour after hour on the training ground the techniques of kicking or passing the ball. A bit of 'visualisation' is not really going to have much impact on players who have been honing and practising these same motor skills from an early age.

As professional coaches, we believe the potential of these proven visualisation techniques has yet to be fully realised in the 'beautiful game'.

As indicted earlier, visualisation has focused narrowly on the physical and technical aspects of the game, for example, taking corners or free-kicks, bending shots and developing accuracy in passing

It is now time to use visualisations for the mental and emotional (psychological) aspects of play, particularly for rehearsing stressful situations of change in a game as well as for developing a stronger sense of common purpose and positive team mind-sets.

## "I am the Greatest!"

A supreme exponent of using visualisation for psychological conditioning and self-affirmation is Mohammed ("I am the Greatest") Ali, former and, for many years, undisputed Heavy-Weight Boxing Champion of the World.

In his book, 'I'm a Little Special', he talks about what he calls his 'future history' and his strong sense of destiny and legacy to boxing.

Ali used visualisations in a very unique and special way to strengthen his confidence and mindset prior to a fight. He developed a detailed picture during his training sessions on how he imagined the fight, from the starting sequence of arriving at the changing rooms prior to the fight to each round of the fight and finishing with the predicted knock-out and count down of his opponent. His powerful imagery would include 'hot' (emotive) words and details of sounds and smells would be included to assemble a realistic, compelling and very personal picture. He would replay this visualisation over and over in his mind's eye and freeze it at significant moments so he could actually examine his emotional experience at those moments, e.g. 'the opponent on the ropes in Round 3'.

He believed completely in his visualisations and communicated them to his camp and fans so lucidly that they believed in them too. He then behaved and acted as though the future he was imagining was already here and now.

The value of such striking psychological visualisations was apparent in the fearsome and 'unbeatable' reputation as a fighter that Ali earned from his opponents and the unshakeable self-confidence and belief he had in his own ability to win.

Visualisations don't just work for individual sportsmen and women. There is a growing body of evidence of their effectiveness in building the right mental mind-sets for sports teams, although so far their use has been largely promulgated in the USA and Canada particularly in American Football and Ice Hockey.

## Too trans-Atlantic?

Fantastic examples of using team visualisation for outstanding results can be found in Sir Clive Woodward's book, 'Winning', in which he describes coaching the England rugby team to victory in the Rugby World Cup in 2003.

These methods are proven in a European context, so here then, are some approaches to mental conditioning for the England Football Team through the power of team visualisation:

- As part of the preparation and build-up to a match, create a compelling full team visualisation prior to a game that takes the team through a winning sequence in as much detail as possible. Create a full picture including the use of all senses and emotions of the team. Encourage the team members to express how they feel, particularly their feelings of winning and successful game-plays and how they overcome anxieties and fears through positive mind-body actions.
- Visualising individual plays during opponent research: allow time for members of the team to share their visualisations of their opponents with other supporting players and with the Coach. Facilitation would be

required to draw out these visualisations in sufficiently realistic detail. Then encourage the players to visualise and imagine successful plays against such an opponent, using videotape of the opposing player as the basis for projection, e.g. how an attacker can out-smart a defender of the opposing team or a defensive back-line can neutralise the threat posed by the opposition's best striker.

- In rehearsing set-pieces on the practise ground, use visualisation of different football situations to develop positive mind-set, mental toughness and self-belief in dealing with:
    - Penalties or, to reframe them, 'set goal-scoring opportunities',
    - Tactical formations
    - Switches of formations
    - Free kicks, corners and other dead-ball situations
    - Disputed refereeing decisions
    - Aggressive play and effective responses
    - Red-card exits and re-grouping by the team (although red cards will be a thing of the past once the team have read this book!)
    - Communication on the field between players

In fact, anything that is relevant to improving team performance, even, we suggest, how to celebrate scoring goals!

- Keep visualisations positive at all times and avoid 'psyching-out' players by imagining situations which show a player constantly 'messing-up' or making mistakes as this can only serve to hurt their game (and their self-confidence!).
- After each game and during team reviews, capture positive moments of performance as visualisations and replay them in future training sessions. We close this chapter with 2 fictional examples of visualisation, of taking a penalty, which illustrate the differences between a negative and a positive mind-set. Another way of viewing these visualisations is as a before and after sequence following a process of one-to-one coaching to elaborate a player's visualisation skills and develop a winning mentality.

## The Longest Walk

You can't believe it, why did the coach ask you? You're not even a midfielder; you shouldn't be expected to take a penalty. Why did he have to ask, why, in front of the others? If he had been discreet you could have made excuses, perhaps mumbled something about a strain.

Oh you idiot, why didn't you simulate an injury five minutes before the final whistle? But now you've been asked, asked in front of the others, so there's no way you could pass, and now you have started to walk, started THE walk, across grass that minutes ago was bright green in the afternoon sunlight, now you don't see the colour, only the penalty spot a long way ahead, further than the edge of the swimming pool, that day as a kid when you almost drowned.

There is nothing, no noise from the crowd permeates your hearing, only the muted sound of your heavy feet, the pulsing of blood through your veins and the incessant questions. Which side does the goalie prefer?

If only you had paid attention, where should I aim the ball? You shuffle up to the spot, the referee speaks, you don't hear it, it was probably the last rites, you are going to let the team down, let the supporters down, let the manager down. Why oh why did he pick you? It is his fault.

The referee steps back, oh no, too soon, you haven't had time to plan this. The goalie is huge; there is so little space to either side of him. You step back, are my laces tight? You run up. No the run up feels wrong, you are going to slice this, it is going to miss, your boot hits the ball. It is too obvious within that instant that you have scuffed it, the ball sails over the crossbar and it's all over.

## Path of Glory

The coach didn't have to ask, you implored him, and he didn't take any persuading. He knows you are one of his best players. With a wink and a grin he jokes "No fancy stuff", and with a pat on the back you are off at a brisk pace across the emerald green sea of grass. The crowd is cheering, you lap it up, they are going to see a wonder goal, what a treat for them. You look up to the stand and smile. What a moment, what an opportunity.

And then you are there, the ref comes up, you see how nervous he looks, you crack a joke, he chuckles appreciatively. You look up at the goalie. He doesn't look nervous, he looks downright scared. You make eye contact. He's doomed, you know his game, you know where to place the ball, you take a moment to visualise the ball, leaving your boot and arching into the top right corner, you rerun the image one more time.

Then just for a moment you allow yourself to think of the game, how well you and the team have played and the games before that. You're good, frankly you deserve to win, really it should never have come to penalties, but since it has.

You step back and with that signature short run up that you have practised consistently during the week, you strike the ball.

Annoyingly, it isn't exactly like your visualisation, it didn't arc quite as much, you'll have to work on that. Still it's in the back of the net as it should be, and with a delighted punch of the air you jog back to the team to offer encouragement to your team's next scorer.

*"What we see depends mainly on what we look for"*

— Sir John Lubbock

## Chapter 12:

# Questions that change mindsets

### Key Area 6: How asking the right questions can challenge thinking and overcome limiting beliefs to move the team forward...

- What's stopping England from winning the World Cup?
- What really needs to happen for England to win the World Cup?
- How does a winning World Cup team perform?
- What could England do differently next time to ensure success?
- What is the key to having a winning mentality?

## The Power of a Question

Asking powerful questions is key to unleashing potential. By asking the right questions and becoming curious about themselves and their performance, players can realise their full abilities both on and off the pitch.

Having looked at visualisation and the need for players to create images and pictures of their desired outcomes in their minds eye, we are now going to build on that, by exploring the types of questions the England players need to ask themselves, or be asked to overcome the limiting beliefs, fears and assumptions that are holding them back from the best performances of their lives. Consideration needs to be given to the questions that are asked in the locker room before the match, at half time, post-match performance and on the pitch. To become the best that they can ever be – The World's Greatest!, England must ensure constant and never ending improvement takes place.

## Exercising the Listening Muscle

It is important that before we address asking powerful question's, we first pay close attention to the skill of active listening. How many of us really take the time out to listen to ourselves? It is not enough just to ask questions, the players need to train their listening muscle and really focus on listening to their inner voice and the answers they receive, even if the response is not what they want to hear.

- What am I doing to make this team achieve better results?
- How can I improve my performance to score more goals?

Being truly listened to is extremely empowering. A Coach who actively listens without interruption, honours and respects your answers, encouraging more from you than you think is possible.

Listening is an undervalued skill, so to the England team, we request that as another part of your fitness regime, please exercise this muscle too and actively listen to the responses you get.

This is ultimately the only way effective change can take place (we deal with effectively managing change in the next chapter). We all have within us, the power to answer every question we are asked. What the England team must do is begin asking themselves powerful questions that really make them STOP and THINK! This frees space for transformation to take place.

"Listening of this calibre ignites the human mind. The quality of your attention determines the quality of other people's thinking". Nancy Kline, Time to Think

The good, the bad and the potentially ugly answer!

Let's explore.... what happens if you ask yourself a bad question?

Err...You may get a bad answer!

Let's imagine what questions players may be asking themselves before taking a penalty...

- What if I miss?
- What will the crowd think?

Here the focus is on missing and what the crowd is thinking. Whatever is in the forefront of the player's mind will influence the outcome of any actions they are taking. Thereby, in the first example, focusing on 'missing' could lead to missing, thus creating a self-fulfilling prophecy. The second example gives the crowd's thoughts uppermost priority in the player's mind, taking focus away from the task in hand. Instead of considering the consequences of missing or of what the crowd are thinking, the player needs to ensure that he is asking himself better focused positive questions, which might be...

- Where do I need to aim to strike the ball into the back of the net?
- What do I need to focus on to score a goal?

Here the attention is directed to aiming, striking, and focusing. These questions give the player clarity and control of the action being taken. The priority is placed on what needs to happen to achieve the desired result, so that there is only the option for a positive outcome – There is no room for failure here.

## Provocative Questions Raise Awareness

A powerful question is designed to provoke a higher quality of thinking, increasing the player's awareness and self-discovery at a whole new level. It gives the opportunity for wider scope of thought, leading to revelation and natural, effortless improvements taking place. The player owns his response, rather than being told what he must do. By owning our decisions, there is greater motivation, responsibility and commitment to take the required action.

Let's examine some different types of questioning techniques that will benefit the England team...

## Questions that... Challenge a player's thinking

- What is it to be an exceptional England Football player?
- What are the expectations of the players and of the team?

To make changes a player needs to have their thinking challenged. When a powerful question is used to do this, it is likely to stop them in their tracks and disturb their current thought pattern. This type of question invites the player to step back from his situation and explore an area from a new perspective, enabling them to think about what's important to them and what it is they really want.

## Questions that... Follow Interest, direct attention and open new perspectives

An example dialogue between a Coach and a Player:

**Coach:** What is it you notice most about how you kick the ball?

**Player:** When I take a penalty, I always seem to strike the ball with the right side of my boot, which makes the ball swerve over to the right.

**Coach:** What else do you notice?

**Player:** When I make clean contact with the ball, it puts a slight spin on it

**Coach:** Describe how it spins?

**Player:** Interesting question! I think it seems to spin faster, when I just clip the side, whereas when I make clean contact with the ball it has a slower more controlled spin. I hadn't really thought about it like this before...

**Coach:** What else do you notice?

**Player:** The sound of my foot on the ball – It is really clear and crisp when I take a great shot and quite a dull thud when I get the wrong angle.

**Coach:** You've mentioned 3 things: the ball swerving; the ball spinning and the sound the ball makes. Which would be the most useful to tackle first?

**Player:** The way the ball spins – I've not really thought too much about that before.

**Coach:** How about you shoot some more balls at the net and tell me what you notice about the spin after each one. (The player's awareness of what he is doing will now be heightened after each shot he takes. He will begin to gain more control of the ball).

Directing attention towards what interests a player opens up different thought processes and new learning. The player may be locked into one way of thinking. Focusing questions on the elements of their current situation that interests them will redirect their thinking patterns and open their mind to new perspectives. People tend to learn more when they have an interest in something; directing the attention to what interests the player assists their learning to open up new possibilities and more resources. (For more information in this area, Timothy Gallway's books, The Inner Game series are excellent)

## Questions that... Pre-suppose

- When you have scored from the penalty spot, how will you celebrate?

This question removes the doubt of 'whether' the action will happen or not. The use of 'When' gives the sense of a definite occurrence rather than an uncertain one. The question also moves the player's thinking on, by presupposing that not only will the player score but will also celebrate.

This type of questioning has the impact on the player of removing barriers to thinking and enables a change of mindset to believe that things are possible. By presupposing, we bypass any barriers that the mind may put up, instinctively freeing it to be open to all options and possibilities in response to the question asked.

## Incisive Questions that overturn Limiting Beliefs

There are many examples of limiting beliefs we could show here, let's take the following one, as an example...

*'England only ever get as far as the quarter finals'*

Here the focus is on only getting as far as the quarter finals. It seems this belief is shared and reinforced by the whole nation – The media, the commentators, the fans, the list goes on....

Chris Waddle, BBC Five Live Sport is quoted as saying:

"We haven't played well, we had years to prepare and nothing's changed, we are a quarter-final team and no more.

"Every time we play a team with a bit of craft and skill we can't deal with it.

"We have got to face reality that we are a team nowhere near the top seven countries in the world".

Time to turn this belief that 'England only ever get as far as the quarter finals' on it's head and ask the following incisive question...

- If England knew they could win the semi-final, what will their strategy be for winning the World Cup Final?

An 'incisive' question queries or negates the validity of a limiting belief. By side stepping the belief and posing the question in such a way, the incisive question invites a new way of thinking. The focus is placed on the second half of the question – the part that requires consideration of what is possible, when the limiting belief is absent, in this instant winning the World Cup. Using an incisive question to challenge a limiting belief, places the emphasis on the positive in a situation.

Throughout the pages of this book we have given many examples of limiting beliefs that the England team and nation are holding. Here are a couple more examples of incisive questions to build the momentum to change these mindsets...

- If you knew you were the World's greatest, how will you perform?
- When you know you will win the World Cup, what will your next goal be?

Both of these questions could be asked, however note that the second one progresses the player's thinking even wider, by suggesting that winning the World Cup is already a given and the focus is now on achievements beyond this.

## Questions are the Answer

We have highlighted elsewhere in our book, various ways of using questions to attain desired results. For example, building a common vision and creating a motivational environment require the right questions to be asked to open up the mind to new options not previously considered. We also point out in our chapter on Vision and Goal-Achievement, the need for performance review. Asking powerful questions following a match or a tournament can really consolidate not only the lessons learned and what could be done differently, but also what went well and the outstanding achievements of the game. It is through asking questions that the team are able to recognise success (we will expand on this in our chapter on Celebrating Success).

- How will we know when we are successful?
- What will be different for us when we are successful?
- How will success feel for us?

In summary, questioning is an extremely effective tool when used regularly by the Coach and Players to open new perspectives, new thought patterns and to discover which areas most require change. When greater awareness of necessary change occurs, this will propel the team to action.

*"We can't solve problems by using the same kind of thinking we used when we created them."*

— Albert Einstein

## Chapter 13:

# Managing change

### Key Area 7: How to develop an effective strategy for managing change to produce winning results

In this chapter, we explore the subject of managing change and examine some of the lessons we can learn from England's World Cup experience. A number of key points emerge on how to manage change more effectively.

But first what do we mean by managing change?

Change in football is exciting and can happen very rapidly, both on and off the field. It is the dynamic ingredient and source of the adrenalin rush for many spectators and is part of the continuing fascination with the game.

For a performing team, however, change can be hazardous and how it is managed can mean the difference between success and failure.

Managing change is not about reacting to events on the field. Effective change management is a fluid process involving such activities as deployment of resources, planning, risk assessment, decision-making, communication and leadership of change. As we have already demonstrated, a strategy for change will include a vision and set of goals with a plan of action to move the team in the right direction.

Implementing change should follow a sequence of PLAN-DO-REVIEW. In other words, you plan the change required, you carry out the change, and you review the results and adapt your plan for further change improvement. A team needs to have in place an effective set of principles for managing change, both for changes which form part of a bigger master plan (strategic change) and for when things don't go according to plan (operational change).

## When it all goes horribly wrong!

One of the enduring images of England's' failure in the World Cup campaign of 2006 were the TV pictures of the England dugout early in the quarter-final game against Portugal in the Veltins Arena, Gelsenkirchen on 1st July 2006.

On the field things were not going according to plan, particularly the change in tactical formation to 4-5-1 (4 defenders, 5 midfielders and 1 striker), which left Wayne Rooney up front in a lone-striker role supported by link-up play from the 5 mid-field players. The delivery of the ball from the England midfield was not getting through to Rooney who looked stranded and increasingly frustrated, left chasing long hopeful passes and effectively marked out of the game by the Portuguese defence.

Sven Goran Eriksson, the England Head Coach, sits impassively, shoulders hunched, staring at his notes, head down, looking tense but detached.

Meanwhile, Steve McClaren runs up and down the touchline waving his arms and imploring the under-performing midfield players to make more effort. Apart from a picture of contrasting leadership styles (of which we will have more to say later), the image says a lot about change and how it can all go horribly wrong if it is not effectively managed.

Outlined below is our guide to the essentials of managing change drawn from some of the best (and worst) practises that we have observed during this and previous World Cups.

## Know when not to change

Before heading off into the management of change, it is worth keeping in mind the old adage: 'If it ain't broke, don't fix it'.

Our most successful England Manager, Sir Alf Ramsey, famously commented, "don't change a winning team". Ramsey stuck by his original team selection for the Wembley Final in 1966: the 11 players that had got England to a place in the World Cup Final. He resisted tremendous media and public pressure to play Jimmy Greaves, the 'Wayne Rooney' of his day, who was recovering from injury for most of the 1966 Tournament but only regained fitness and was available to play in the Final.

Of course, the emphasis, here, is on 'a winning team': the fact that the current England team is well short of greatness in performance terms makes the argument for change self-evident! However, before embarking on any change programme, it is important to recognise and value what is working and seek to retain it (see also our chapter on success where we have identified some of the successes in the England team's performances in 2006).

**Have a strategic plan for change and then follow it 'before' considering alternative options.**

Responsibility for change, particularly tactical and strategic change, lies usually with the head coach and is an aspect of the modern football coach's job description that is guaranteed to set tongues wagging amongst football fans and the pundits. Sir Alf Ramsey caused a storm of controversy when he took over as England Manager in 1964 and introduced his 'daring' 4-4-2 formation (4 defenders, 4 midfielders, 2 attackers) for the team who emerged 2 years later as successful World Cup holders and became known as 'the wingless wonders'. The formation took time to gel and it was only through determination, persistence and practice to a plan that it eventually paid off.

Sven's reputation as a sophisticated tactical egg-head may have survived after the 2006 World Cup but his switching of formations between games (4-4-2 to the experimental 'Diamond' of 3-1-5-1 to 4-5-1) and constant tinkering created an impression of indecisiveness, lack of conviction and poor planning. The World Cup tournament was not the right place to be experimenting with new changes or unfamiliar roles for players and team alike. It would have been far more effective to have experimented, tested and mastered or, where appropriate, rejected such formations as part of a strategic master plan for change prior to Germany 2006.

To put it another way:

*"If you are leaping a ravine, the moment of takeoff is a bad time to be considering alternative strategies."*

— British comedian and writer, John Cleese (born 1939)

As part of your plan, make sure you have adequate resources to facilitate change and a back-up plan when you do not.

The England head coach's decision to include the untried 17 year-old Theo Walcott in the England World Cup squad, as if 'to make up the numbers' as one football-writer suggested, backfired and appears a reckless gamble in hindsight. When Michael Owen limped out of the tournament, Sven's options for change in his attacking formation narrowed: they were fatally impaired after Rooney's exit, even though England supporters were mercifully spared the embarrassment of a semi-final featuring Peter Crouch as England's one remaining proven striker.

There also appeared to have been a lack of contingencies for change in Sven's planning. Where was Plan B or C when Plan A was clearly not working? What might have been a better or alternative use of the resources at the head coach's disposal?

In contrast, Marcello Lippi, the Italian team's head coach, seems to have given himself plenty of attacking options (6 strikers in his squad for Germany) and a range of contingencies in his tactical formations. He made maximum use of his squad during the tournament, fielding every player apart from his two substitute goalkeepers.

## Monitor your plan and act decisively when things aren't working!

When players weren't performing (England's Frank Lampard and David Beckham were 2 notable examples by common consent), Sven resisted making a change intervention, offering instead feeble suggestions that performances would improve by the next game!

Sir Alf Ramsey expected his players to perform at every game and dropped or substituted them immediately when they didn't, regardless of their 'reputation'.

There are further examples of avoidance of managing change by the England head coach. It had been clear for some time prior to the tournament that playing Steven Gerrard and Frank Lampard together in similar midfield roles was not working, a pairing which seemed to neutralise their undoubted individual attacking talents. Sven obstinately refused to accept the necessity for a strategic change in the pairing of the 2 midfielders. As Martin Jol, the then Tottenham manager and professional Dutchman, commented in his column on Sven's dilemma at the time:

*"He (Sven) has to be brave, which means getting his strongest team out on the pitch—and that's not necessarily the same as simply picking your best 11 players."*

Marcello Lippi had no fear of change. Big-name players like Francesco Totti and Alessandro Del Piero were not guaranteed a place in the starting 11 at the World Cup, with Lippi keeping faith with Serie A's top scorer Luca Toni. Fellow strikers Alberto Gilardino, Filippo Inzaghi and Vincenzo Iaquinta were used depending on what was best for the team, not the ego or success of the player. The out-of-form Vieri was not even given a plane ticket. In one of his press interviews, he said:

*"No-one is guaranteed a place. All the players have to do well game after game-that is the way things are."*

## Assess and accept the level of risk and then take action which is most likely to be successful.

Making changes involves managing risk. Risk has been defined as 'a chance or possibility of danger, loss, injury or other adverse consequences' (Concise Oxford English Dictionary 8th Edition). It is not always guaranteed that a planned action, however well-conceived, will be effective. The factors that will determine success and failure have to be calculated and taken into account if a situation requiring decisive change is to be managed effectively. Their effects have to be minimised or optimised. For example, a key substitution may significantly alter the course of a game depending on the timing, the team's performance and the readiness of the player as well as the opposing team's deployment.

A decision involving risk will always be a calculation, a judgement call by the coach and because there is uncertainty there is always the possibility that the change will fail.

Of course, the chances of success are much greater if the above points about planning, availability of resources and recognition that change is necessary have been followed.

In addition to these principles, though, the level of risk has to be managed and understood.

Some of Sven's tactical changes and substitutions appear with the benefit of hindsight to reveal an attitude to risk which was strategically cautious and defensive, to the point of attempting to eliminate risk, and where resources were focused to neutralise and cancel out threats posed by the opposition.

The football objective was 'not-to-lose' by not conceding goals, slowing down the play to break up opponents' rhythm, looking to gain and exploit dead-ball situations as the route to goal, stifling the play in the middle of the field etc.

*"One hundred percent of the shots you don't take don't go in."*

— Wayne Gretzky, Canadian Ice Hockey Player

The opposite approach to risk is to have a more open, freer attitude to and tolerance of risk and to deploy resources to their best advantage, playing to the team's strengths and positive attributes. Where, for example, the football objective is to win by scoring goals, attacking and creating goal-scoring chances in the last 3rd of the pitch and looking for penetrating runs to keep the other team in their own half while keeping possession of the ball.

Managing risk in this way embraces uncertainty rather than runs away from it and at the same time balances risk with reward. It is a winner's strategy: permitting and nurturing a freer expression of a team's footballing values, releasing the creative potential of winning plays and actually producing better football from a spectators' point of view!

We are not saying that a coach should ignore risk (successful teams in Germany 2006 were built on strong, well-organised defences): we are saying that in taking decisions involving change, there is a balancing act between risk and reward which calls for these things to achieve the greater prize:

- Realistic judgement (what do I know/ what do I not know?)
- Flexibility (play safe or play to win) and
- Timing (when is the best time for change to succeed?)

Lippis' tactical switch and higher stakes gamble to unleash 4 attackers in the closing stages of the semi-final against Germany is a fantastic example of effective change-management where accepting a higher level of risk in order to score within free-play brought its just rewards! Lippi recognised that, with the clock running down in extra time, there was an increasing probability that the game would be decided on a penalty shoot-out, which, given their previous record and home advantage, would favour the German team. He calculated that the best option of success was to commit his team to all out attack in the closing period of the game. Lippi took the gamble which won the jackpot. His substitutions produced the winning goals that secured a place for the 'Azzurri' in the World Cup Final in Berlin!

In contrast, one of the biggest blunders of change management where the level of risk was miscalculated in Germany 2006 has to be the decision by the Argentine coach, Jose Peckerman, to take off their best player – gifted playmaker Juan Roman Riquelme - with half an hour to go when leading Germany 1-0 in their quarter final match. The defensive move (Riquelme was replaced by a defender), while obviously executed according to a pre-conceived tactical plan (Riqueleme was not injured), was mistimed and under-estimated the risks. The switch in tactics effectively surrendered mid-field possession to the German team who got back into the game, equalised and eventually went on to defeat Argentina on penalties.

Communicate the need for change and make sure everyone understands the reasons and the benefits.

When preparing a team for change it is essential that the team is clear about the reasons for change, understands it and is allowed to express concerns and anxieties, find answers to their questions, and appreciate the benefits.

In an interview after the World Cup, John Terry, the England centre-back, admitted that in the England dressing room team-talks "in my personal opinion ...we've been a little bit inside ourselves. We all need to come out of our shells and not be scared".

No amount of shouting and external pressure will work if the players' thoughts, individually or as a team, are not aligned in a positive direction towards change. Communication has not worked if behaviour hasn't changed or if people are silent, uneasy or sceptical about the benefits.

Lampards' faint-hearted comments after the Ecuador game about the lone striker role that Rooney was adapting to are suggestive that some self-convincing is still going on:

*"I thought Rooney did well against Ecuador and grew into the role as the game went on... People might question him playing up front on his own when he's used to coming off people – but he's got the ability to do whatever he wants. He will improve. Its not easy when you've been out for a couple of months and you're coming back at the top level, but ...he will get stronger."*

In his World Cup diary on msn.com, after his untimely return home from Germany and prior to the Portugal game, Michael Owen was more forthright and was quick to record his own misgivings about Sven's tactical formation of 4-5-1:

*"If I was playing, there's not much I could do there either because we're not whizzing crosses in, we're not playing great through balls or anything like that... I always like 2 players up front, it gives you options and they can feed off each other."*

It is a leader's role to inspire confidence and lead change, by inspiring passion, commitment and purpose

Brian Clough of Nottingham Forest once cheekily commented on the FA's appointment of Sven Goran Erickson. "At last", he said, "England have appointed a manager who speaks English better than the players".

However good his mastery of our native language may have been, Sven's inability to rouse his players to change when it mattered most, was an unequivocal failure of leadership.

Sven's touchline behaviour lacked the passion to inspire players. Steve McClaren was the man running around yelling at the highly paid but unproductive players.

How Sven came across to his players in their team-talks we can only infer but a comment by John Terry, the England centre-back, after the World Cup is engagingly diplomatic in its economy of expression:

*"He (Sven) was a little bit quiet... I prefer a Manager who is in your face."*

It also recalls the comment of Gareth Southgate, a former England player, on Sven's team-talk at half-time in the 2002 World Cup quarter-final against Brazil (Leading 1-0, England lost 2-1):

*"We were expecting Winston Churchill and instead got Iain Duncan Smith."*

To be effective, the leader must consider the emotional aspect in the message of change and its impact on players. Words that contain inspiration, vitality and excitement open up the mind to new possibilities and pathways for action, to reframe situations as opportunities or chances to succeed and win.

Resignation, scepticism and anxiety focus thinking in other directions and permit the possibility of failure. We would add that quiet logic, however nicely expressed, just numbs the mind and produces indifference and apathy!

Another post-World Cup story, told by Steve McClaren, makes the point eloquently:

*"Becks had given a little talk, then opened it up for anyone else and in came JT (John Terry), effing this and blinding that, and afterwards Sven turned round and said, 'You wouldn't get John Terry in a church, would you?"*

Who was the real leader in this situation? Who was expressing the passion and modelling the commitment and purpose that was required to lead the change in the players' performance?

So far, in this chapter, we have put all the responsibility on the Coach to manage change effectively, whether changes are strategic or operational, pro-active or re-active. It should be remembered, however, that in football it's the players who have to take on and 'be' the change on the pitch.

## Develop the right attitudes to change

It's how we choose to react to change that determines the effectiveness of our response and subsequent behaviour. The wrong attitude will undermine any possibility of change succeeding, however rational or necessary the change appears to be.

For example, there seemed a worrying lack of commitment to Sven's changes in tactics to the lone striker role: we question whether the players understood the need for change or were convinced of the benefits. How did they choose to react to yet another tactical switch? How did their re-action (doubt/ mistrust/ lack of confidence/ anger) determine their subsequent actions (attempts at long balls/ misplaced passes/ lack of goal attempts or real penetration into their opponent's half of the field)?

Even if they understood the logic for a tactical change, how far did they believe in its effectiveness or were committed to their own ability to execute the change?

Michael Owen, in an interview with ITV, was quick to defend Wayne Rooney's reaction (stamping on the Portuguese defender, Ricardo Carvalho) and subsequent sending-off:

*"He probably only got angry because of what happened in the first hour. It's a frustrating role to play. Wayne is one of the best strikers in the world and you're cutting one of his legs off if you play one up front."*

To succeed, players, as well as coaches, have to develop a different attitude to change.

Every player has to understand their role and the job that is being asked of them on the pitch. They also need to have expressed their reaction and aligned their attitude to that role particularly where change or uncertainty in a new role is concerned. It goes without saying, that it is preferable that such reactions are managed prior to, rather than during, performance.

## Study when change is effective and learn how to replicate it.

The England 'Dunkirk' performance against Portugal in Gelsenkirchen is not the only example of a team that was reduced to 10 men in the competition in Germany and had to re-organise and grapple with the challenge of sudden and unexpected change on the pitch. A remarkable example of how to cope effectively with the same 10 man scenario is provided by the eventual champions, Italy, in their quarter final game with Australia. The key difference is that the Italians succeeded and pulled off a famous victory. Why?

All of the above change management principles were followed and applied:

- There was a strategy for change introduced 2 years previously by Lippi when he took over after the 'catastrofe' of Euro 2004
- There were a number of tactical formations rehearsed and executed to plan prior to the tournament. Lippi knew what worked and what didn't before their arrival in Germany
- Change decisions were taken 'decisively' and for the good of the overall team. Every player was treated in the same way and was regarded as only as good as their last performance
- Resources were balanced between attacking and defensive options and utilised to the full
- Risks were calculated and balanced with what was required to achieve success and when to apply change. Italy's late winning penalty against Australia came as a result of consistent pressure and commitment to attack in the final part of the game
- Every member of the team knew what was expected of them and was motivated to adapt to whatever was expected of them for the team's success
- Lippi instilled in the team an iron will and self –belief that they could only succeed, whatever the odds

- They learned from each game and made the necessary changes for improvement

Italy's win, like their other performances in the 2006 World Cup, was no fluke. Like the tip of an iceberg, it was built upon an effective change management process that had commenced 2 years previously, a steady and deliberate accretion of planned changes as part of an over-arching change strategy. With the right foundations in place, it is possible for a team to overcome the threat of unexpected defeat, to adapt, innovate and succeed in spite of the odds: England needs to study and learn from such examples.

## Time to drop the dead donkey of 'Self-fulfilling Prophecy'

As a nation of football fans, we recognise that it is also time to change and move on. We need to jettison our traditional and passive acceptance of the outcome of our national team's performance as always the same, as part of a continuing 'inevitable' pattern. We need to stop wallowing in self-pity, recalling a tragic cycle of glorious failures when things didn't go our way 'yet again'. We need to quit blaming our shortcomings on being, to quote Sven, "a little bit unlucky".

Let us study and learn from our past but not remain a prisoner to it.

Thorough and comprehensive change is imperative for the England team. Change is required at both strategic (team direction/ vision/ values and belief system) and operational (tactical/ preparation and planning /goal setting and leadership/ performance) levels. We have described in detail elsewhere in this book, what those changes might look like.

Implementing the change process and managing the results will be the greatest test of the coaching team. By applying all of the above change management principles, many of the pitfalls and mistakes of the past will be avoided. Only then, will an England team be ready to face the challenge of change with total confidence and take control of their own destiny.

*"A pessimist sees the difficulty in every opportunity. An optimist sees the opportunity in every difficulty."*

— Sir Winston Churchill (1874-1965)

# Chapter 14:

# A contract with the fans

## Key Area 8: How, by building trust, developing mutual respect and sharing expectations, the fans can help create England's successful future...

How can fans become more involved in the success of a team? Well in order to examine the possibilities, let's first consider an imaginary dialogue between the Spirit of the England Football Team and Joe Public, the voice of the England fans:

**England:** Excuse me. Do you have five minutes? I really need to talk to you about something that is important to me.

**Joe:** Can't you see I'm busy? Wimbledon has started and I've got to watch Henman and Murray fall off their pedestals.

**England:** Well it's along those lines that I'd like to have this chat. Please, just five minutes of your time.

**Joe:** Five minutes of time. What's that worth to you? £100,000, £200,000 or more? It's alright when you want something of me, how about when I want something from you?

**England:** Tell me.

**Joe:** What?

**England:** Tell me. If this is going to be worthwhile, to both of us, I need to know and understand what you want from me.

**Joe:** Alright then, but you're not going to like it. May I bring to your attention the blog entry by someone calling themselves Leadguy007, I think it just about sums up how a lot of us feel:

*"Even in the cold light of day, I cannot bring myself to forgive the millionaire failures that have destroyed a country's dream. It is not enough anymore to say that "we are just not good enough", that's bo*****s, we have some of the best players in the world. No, what we do not have is heart. Did you watch Australia, they chased every single ball, they went out, but as heroes. All our lot did was negative, non committed play. Even after scraping by after 120 minutes of this rubbish, all they had to do was score, one on one, from 12 yards and they couldn't do that. Rooney's sending off was typical of the selfish, playboy, sulky attitude of all of our 'superstars'. Hang your head in shame, you didn't train hard enough, you didn't play hard enough, you weren't as passionate as the fans that cheered you on, and you did this with your Nation watching. I don't know how you can live with yourselves."*

**England:** Well, that was to the point. All we had to do was score – ah! It's all clear to me now. When I'm on the pitch I try to focus on the game but I'm only human and sometimes the pressure gets to me. What I would like at those times is for the crowd to help with my confidence levels not destroy what little still remains. You mentioned the passion "of the fans that cheered (us) on".

Well, they don't cheer all the time. Why do you have to boo me and jeer? Why call for me to be taken off? Do you think this helps?

**Joe:** It helps me release my frustration at the fact you're paid all that money, lead a lifestyle I can only dream of, yet you don't seem to give a damn as to whether you win or not. The two hours I spend in the stadium, what with all the travel, buying a programme, eating a hotdog and paying for the actual ticket costs me almost a week's wages. It means a lot to me. I'd like to see more dedication coming from you. I want to be there. I want to cheer you on but sometimes I get so depressed. On paper England has one of the best midfields but other teams just seem to frustrate us. On paper we have a dire reputation for scoring penalties so why not win games and avoid this nightmare? No wonder we all start booing - utter frustration.

Maybe we're setting our expectations too high? Perhaps the fans, like the players, should just be content to reach the quarter finals. Perhaps if we all have this as our goal we won't be so disappointed.

**England:** I'm not content to settle for a quarter final placement but maybe expectations aren't always as realistic as they could be. Excellent players don't always make an excellent team. You only have to look at Real Madrid to understand this. They've bought all the supposedly top players in the world – Figo, Beckham, Zidane and what have they won? Diddly squat! Maybe if you could show a little bit more faith in me I would raise my game, as I would really want to do well for you, and if I can believe that you believe in me, I'd feel stronger.

**Joe:** So it's my fault?

**England:** No, I'm not saying that. Can we please move away from a blame culture and look at what we can both do, that will result in a win/ win situation?

**Joe:** OK. Let me see if I've got this straight. England are playing like a load of donkeys but rather than boo and hiss, which is my natural reaction, I should cheer you on saying things like 'Come on son, I know you can do it'.

**England:** Exactly.

**Joe:** But it's like you said earlier, it's down to both of us. You can't ask me to stop saying you're useless if you don't stop saying the same thing to yourself.

**England:** Point taken. If we all commit to a positive viewpoint we're a step closer to achieving our joint aim.

**Joe:** Ah, but there you are again, a joint aim? We don't feel there is one. I want to have something to believe in. I want to be proud of my team, of being English. I love all the flags flying from bedroom windows and car aerials. I want to be one of the fans of the winning team.

**England:** But you're contradicting yourself. You've just used the example of Australia as a team to be admired and they didn't win. Playing your heart out doesn't always mean you'll win.

**Joe:** I know, but you do neither. Look, I put a huge amount of effort into being an England fan but don't see you putting quite so much effort into being an England player. It's almost as if it doesn't matter to you. Perhaps, because you're such hugely successful people in other areas, what with all your advertising endorsements and TV appearances, you just don't need the added success of winning the World Cup.

**England:** One of the things I have learned recently is that my goal as an England player in the world cup is to win. All of us need this as the purpose that unites us. It's not enough to have a dream to be picked for the team or to play in the team. We must desire to win.

**Joe:** You're suggesting we're all united in our aim but we still need to get over the 'them and us' thing going on between fans and players.

**England:** What do you mean?

**Joe:** Years ago when my Dad took me to football, the players came from the people. They related to them. You'd see them down the pub. They weren't a bunch of prima donnas going around in designer suits, hiding behind designer sun glasses, with designer girlfriends, posh cars and villas on The Palm, Jumeira, Dubai. Now we've got nothing in common. You sit in your ivory towers and we're still down here on the ground. Look at the way you behaved when you came back to England after the world cup – you landed on the opposite side of the airport to where the loyal fans were waiting and were then spirited away in your chauffeur driven limos.

**England:** Well perhaps we didn't want to be bombarded with eggs and tomatoes.

**Joe:** If you integrated more we'd feel differently.

**England:** So, in your expert opinion, how do we do that?

**Joe:** There you go again, high and mighty. It's not an expert opinion, it's a humble and honest opinion. Talk with your fans, not just at them. Find out what matters to them and address it. Don't whine about the weather and the ref. Play good football and have a positive outlook. Acknowledge us and the part we play. Be seen in the communities, be part of the people.

**England:** That's not fair. Lot's of the players are giving to the community through soccer academies and other charity work. The Professional Footballers Association (PFA) supports a number of charitable establishments. We've donated over £5.8million to the Prince's Trust which aims to motivate young people and develop their confidence. Seventy schools in Tanzania were equipped with books from donations by players to Oxfam last year. We also support other major charities such as the Bobby Moore Fund, Truce International, Children Today, Opportunity International...

**Joe:** That's great and should receive more publicity as the balance between column inches in the press devoted to your good deeds and those devoted to the social whirls of your life are disproportionate.

**England:** That's the press' fault not ours.

**Joe:** There you go again. "It's not our fault" Are you telling me you have no clout with the press? Are you telling me you couldn't afford to hire the best PR people? When there's a general election the politicians take to the streets. They understand that it's important the public see them as real people. Take a leaf from their book.

**England:** I get the point, too many shots of us in exotic locations or at press conferences and not enough of us patting dogs and kissing new born babies.

**Joe:** Getting there. So what next?

**England:** You said that it was important that we listened to and acknowledged the fans. You also said that we should align our goals and vision. How does a joint declaration of intent sound to you?

**Joe:** Well if you're up for it I'll give it a go. So, if we had a joint contract, what would it look like?

We, the authors, suggest it would look something like this:

# *Contract*

*We, the undersigned, pledge to develop greater harmony and understanding between the players and supporters of England Football team through mutual agreement on the following issues:*

1. *Committing to a positive view point with both sides believing that success is possible*
2. *The fans will make more use of clapping, cheering and singing uplifting songs and refrain from booing, hissing and jeering*
3. *The players will show more sensitivity to the fans and work to bridge the gap between themselves and their supporters*
4. *The fans will show greater sensitivity to the players and not seek to destroy them*
5. *Good deeds will be given greater focus*
6. *Both fans and players will stop whining*

*Signed...*

Joe Public

Joe Public

The Spirit of the England Team

## Chapter 15:

# Motivational environments

### Key Area 9: How to create an atmosphere that propels the team to exceptional performance time and time again...

If money were no object, technology did not stand in our way and we could indulge our imagination, what kind of environment would we create to stimulate the England team not only to action but to ultimate success?

## New Property! Just on the market – early viewing recommended.

We are pleased to be able to offer an imaginary environment in excellent condition throughout.

The area consists of the following:

Front entrance to Stadium atrium (40,000 square metres including 9,480 square metres of turf), beautifully manicured lawns with clear area delineation. Outstanding overhead lighting capable of illuminating your most glorious experiences. Unique surround sound system transmits uplifting, encouraging and empowering chants and songs wherever you are. Goal nets at each end of the pitch have been lovingly hand-fixed to posts giving optimum taughtness and superb twang effect when hit by balls at speed. Red and white drapery hangs in abundance making the occupier feel truly at home. Stairs to:

Changing room (160 square metres). A brightly lit, luxurious spa awaits your indulgence. The state of the art audio systems can pick up on your psychological needs and provide precisely the music most appropriate to bring you to a complete state of focus and determination. Invigorating aromas pulse at 18 second intervals before games to lift the spirits, whilst soothing fragrances are present post match. If success does have a sweet smell you are bound to experience it here. Softer than soft towels will envelop you after your shower. Steam resistant plasma TV screens will ensure that you are able to view over and over your most memorable positive moments on the pitch. Corridor to:

Tournament accommodation (100 square metres per player). Let your imagination run riot in your private quarters. Close your eyes and imagine a physical environment where you can prepare yourself effortlessly for a campaign to victory. Now open your eyes and look around. Trophies, awards, photos and mementos adorn the walls to provide recognition of your past achievements and inspire.

At the touch of a button, the wall colour will change to provide a hue to meet your required level of mental stimulation. A voice gently whispers how marvelous, outstanding and talented you are or, should you prefer, music will kick start your big match preparation.

The reality is that in these early years of the twenty first century we are not yet able to fully control our environment. Even if we could, we all react differently to stimulus. The role of the WAGS is a prime example. Whilst some players would have found the presence of their nearest and dearest a great inspiration; others would have found this to be a real distraction.

It is vital for any manager to discover what stimulates his players to action at an early stage and then play to this as much as possible.

*"Motivation is an internal state of arousal that often precedes behaviour."*

— Robert Epstein.

With regards to appearing at and doing well in the world cup we need to take this definition further: Motivation is about physical and mental energy being in sync. with action to achieve optimum performance.

This can be demonstrated perfectly if we look at Brazil. Here was a team bursting with self-confidence, belief and skill who could rightly feel they would be in with a fantastic chance of taking the trophy home with them. They played as though a place in the final was theirs regardless of whether they put any effort into their game. They were mistaken. There has to be action!

So, how do you get people to strive to achieve? Control can certainly be exercised over physical energy levels; exercise, diet and sleep all have considerable impact on these. Klinsman, the German manager, was praised for introducing a Californian nutritional package to the German team which appeared to boost the levels of their energy.

However, the successful management of the psychological approach was the common denominator for effective teams at this World cup tournament.

Let's take a look at the possible motivators for teams. What do they seek? Is it celebrity, money and material gain? Whilst Togo seemed to fall apart when payments were not received and accommodation was not up to standard, we can only assume that these factors do not affect the top players who already have wealth and fame in spades.

We need to strip back exactly what the world cup means to the players. It is essential to find the spur, the incentive that will truly get them going. One thing is for sure, if their aim, vision, goal, isn't the most important thing to them, nothing, short of the threat of torture (which we don't recommend as a motivator) will drive them forward.

For those teams – Angola, Trinidad and Tobago, Ghana and Australia to name but a few, whose initial goal was to compete in the World Cup, simply being in Germany for the competition meant they had already succeeded. They could enjoy the experience safe in the knowledge that they had done themselves and their countries proud. Roger Milla and Samuel Eto'o, Cameroon heroes past and present, paid a morale boosting visit to the Ghana players' camp in Germany. Stephen Appiah, Ghana's captain said "The guys are ready to die for the nation. It's a motivating factor for us to show [the world] the kind of football we play in Africa".

Presumably they didn't want to receive any thrashings in the tournament and this may have been a stimulus to play as well as they could. Another motivating factor for individual players may well have been to seize the opportunity of performing on a world stage before the likes of Man. Utd. and Real Madrid's scouts. But here we start to see the dichotomy between team goals and individual purpose. It's more difficult for a manager to motivate a team where he must address a variety of motivators rather than a team with a common purpose. As the competition progressed it became blatantly obvious that those teams united by a common driver were more compelled than those without.

We're talking here particularly about France who were motivated by a common desire to prove wrong their critics who said the team were too old and couldn't score goals and Italy, who wanted to show the world that there was a positive side to Italian football as well as seek atonement for past 'failures'.

*"We've accumulated a lot of anger after two major disappointments,"* Cannavaro, the Italian captain, told the press.

*"First we lost to the host nation in 2002, and that was dubious, and then we failed in Portugal. We've put that rage to good use on the pitch, and you can see that at this World Cup. We're turning this anger into something positive."*

But let's strip motivators back even further and search for some basic human requirements that can be part of every player's make-up and can therefore be more effectively targeted.

Three common human motivators come to mind: to feel valued, to receive recognition and to be part of something.

With so many of the Italian team directly affected by the match fixing scandal back home, it must have been quite a task to keep the players minds from dwelling in a negative way on this unsettling event. Yet Lippi's positive attitude and enthusiasm shone through:

*"I have always considered being leader of this national team to be something magical... for the past two years, I have tried to transmit this feeling to all my players and they have responded with their great enthusiasm."*

The Italian goalie, Gianluigi Buffon reciprocated with:

*"The team spirit is the secret for us to have gone so far – credit has to go to head coach Marcello Lippi who has the tactical quality to bring the best out of the players. He makes every player feel important"*

In the England camp we have to believe that not only was Sven made to feel decidedly unvalued by the FA's decisions on his future but we must also ask how important Sven made each and every one of his players feel.

Clearly we don't know the answer to this but with players such as Owen questioning his decisions and Terry saying that Sven was a little quiet for his liking, we can only assume that the locker room wasn't all it could have been. Perhaps we need look no further than the 'fake sheik' fiasco. Sven 'disclosed' to an undercover reporter posing as a wealthy Arab that he thought Ferdinand was "lazy", Rooney was from a "rough" background and that Michael Owen was "not very" happy at Newcastle. How could players trust their manager after this News of the World sting? How could they reveal to him their fears, concerns or anxieties let alone their hopes and aspirations, knowing that he was capable of repeating these to a complete stranger? His actions would, if nothing else, dampen free expression.

We also have the suspicion that Sven had his favourites, Beckham being the main example, and that often the best players were chosen over the best team. What effect would this have had on the rest of the team? For Lippi, by way of contrast, there were no favoured players, only a favourite team.

Having so many people: media, other managers, commentators, players and fans, criticising does not make for a motivational environment. The England squad, like many other squads, was bombarded from all sides, from within and without. Yet the England team allowed the comments to feed their unease whereas to other teams criticism was like water off a duck's back. We can only assume that where there are already chinks and insecurities it is easier to be affected by harsh comments. John Terry made the comment that "We've all been a bit inside ourselves", which suggests a team with dysfunctional communication processes; players not feeling the confidence to speak up for themselves and displaying low self esteem.

## "All together now"

Being part of something, belonging, is a key motivator. This is why team building is such big business. How big a part psychological team building played during Sven's reign we can only, once again, speculate. What differentiates the league teams from the national side is the stability of a settled squad of players and the consistency of playing together – instinctively knowing where your colleagues are and understanding their capabilities. There was certainly too much churn; selection, reselection and more selection under Sven. Whilst it's essential to try out players and combinations eventually you need to settle on a group who can work as a team. With the England team playing together as a team so infrequently, it is important to consider artificial methods to accelerate team development and bonding. John Terry cites some useful ways in which the 'new' Chelsea was created:

*"We've gone paintballing and go-kart racing. It helps that we're all young lads, that's the key, because there aren't too many old guys around the team these days, well, except for Claude Makelele. And it's important that as many of us as possible do these things. The foreign lads have actually been the most eager, no one makes their excuses and says they're busy."*

Such activities, though fun, have a serious purpose, developing a closer understanding of each other, building relationships, forming alliances and building trust. The England players recognised the talent amongst them but repeatedly made comments that they just weren't gelling as a team.

*"A team is a small group of people with complementary skills and abilities who are committed to a common goal and approach for which they hold each other accountable."*

— Wisdom of Teams

The optimum size for teams, according to the book 'Wisdom of Teams', is 7-12 individuals, so we can tick this box. Undoubtedly the players have the necessary skills and abilities that complement the team's purpose. Not all members have the same skills, but together they are greater than the sum of their parts. Teams identify and reach consensus on their common goals and approaches, rather than looking to a leader to define the goal and approach, as we have mentioned in our chapter on goals. With accountability the team should look to all members to address any performance problems. The very crux of building teams rather than groups of individuals is to get results and achieve victory beyond what would be possible for the individuals working alone. With this in mind it becomes the role of the head coach to facilitate these components; to ensure that the course is set; that appropriate communication exists to convey strategies and objectives, that everyone understands what is being asked of them; that players feel valued. The England team of the future will need to address some serious questions:

- What processes need to be put in place to foster these attributes of a great team?
- How will the team monitor these processes to ensure they work
- What will be their ground-rules and standards to ensure everyone is involved and commitment is high?
- How will skill levels be assessed and performances recognised and rewarded – individually and collectively?

- How can the team gain greater value from the limited time they spend together to develop greater levels of team-focus and understanding?
- How can more time be created?
- How should the head coach address the team, what works and when? Some players will need coaxing whereas others may respond better to 'a kick up the backside'. The head coach must not be afraid to demand excellence

*"I am easily satisfied with the very best."*

— Winston Churchill

And what of the role the fans have to play in all this? Team members and the FA praised the England supporters:

*"England fans are the best supporters in the world. No other country gets the support we do, especially at big tournaments. The fans can really help the team by giving us positive, passionate support."*

— Beckham

However, there was a hollow ring to their comments, or perhaps this was just nervousness in the face of the player's own doubts over their abilities to deliver.

As any of us who had stood among the supporters will know, some fans could, and did, become highly critical and abusive towards the England squad if they felt they had been let down.

That the players were aware and were affected by the fans there is little doubt. As Owen Hargreaves puts it:

*"Ask if you want a boo or a cheer and you always have a cheer."*

What causes detachment between the players and their fans? Well, as with any relationship, there are a host of reasons why this may occur: one feeling the other is not pulling their weight, differences of opinion over what needs to be done and how or an absence of shared dreams.

It would appear that those teams where the manager, players and supporters were in alignment came through much less scathed than our England boys. The effect of this alignment will be picked up again in our next chapter on celebrating success.

To reiterate, motivation at a basic level is driven by the desire for recognition of our efforts, our skill sets, our training and our commitment to a cause. It relies on acknowledgement of our achievements and goals met. It is about belonging to something that gives us value – remaining an individual, detached and outside the unit will not provide the necessary motivational environment that will see the team gel. Post Germany 2006 the England team needs to take time to examine their performances and what didn't work for them. They need to look at the likes of Italy and France and ask themselves what they can learn from these teams. They need to look at their own insecurities and create goals for overcoming these. The England team is fortunate to be entering a new era and we hope that time can be taken during this period to learn from the past yet to focus on the future.

With this in mind, we will take a closer look at celebration – not only of final outcomes but also the efforts made along the way - in the next chapter.

*"People become really quite remarkable when they start thinking that they can do things. When they believe in themselves they have the first secret of success."*

— Norman Vincent Peale

# Chapter 16: Celebrating success

## Key Area 10: How to celebrate each step of success and gain momentum on the road to victory in South Africa 2010...

**success** [s_k séss]

(plural **successes**)

noun

1. **Achievement of desired aim:** the achievement of something planned or attempted
2. **Attainment of fame, wealth, or power:** impressive achievement, especially the attainment of fame, wealth, or power

3. **Something that turns out well:** something that turns out as planned or intended

(Microsoft Encarta)

One of the key elements of goal setting is being able to recognise success when it arrives. As the definitions above imply, success is wrapped up with achievement, attainment and planning. It's not about luck or chance. Although this chapter is entitled 'Celebrating success' it could equally well be entitled 'Setting realistic goals, that are specific, to ensure that you do all the things you need to do, in the right order, within a given time frame, to ensure that at the end of it all you will be able to have one heck of a big party'. Success is the culmination of all the other steps discussed in this book and, having followed all those other stages the least you deserve is a pat on the back.

Success breeds success – the more you succeed, the more evidence you accumulate to prove to yourself and others that you are successful. In turn this promotes greater confidence and self belief which leads to even more success. Easy, all you have to do is jump on the merry-go-round.

It may seem strange but some folk are frightened by success. The internal conversation goes something like this:

- If I succeed people will expect more from me
- I won't be able to meet their expectations
- The pressure will be too much
- Oh heck, I'd be better off not trying at all

Fear of success could be a whole new chapter (or book) but for now we'd like to show how a few well directed questions can go a long way to dispelling this fear. Questions such as:

- What can I do to ensure that expectations are not unrealistic?
- What can I do to better prepare myself to deal with pressure?
- What benefits will success bring to me?

Not 'blowing your own trumpet' is a peculiarly British thing but not taking credit for successes is potentially harmful. If you believe that you were 'lucky', that 'destiny' was on your side or that you were just 'fortunate to be in the right place at the right time', not only are you doing yourself a great disservice but you will not be encouraged to reflect sufficiently on the role you have played. If you cannot analyse performance, skill or learning, you will not develop.

Let's start a campaign right now:

Another 'peculiarly' British trait is that we appear as a nation not to want our heroes to get too big, we enjoy seeing their rise in relation to the scale of their potential fall. We prefer our heroes to be in the mould of Eddie the Eagle – plucky, humorous but failing. Are we witnessing the politics of envy or smugness in our national psyche? Not only do we not seem to want to blow our own trumpets but no-one else wants to blow them either!

In the US they love their heroes and champion success. Whilst failure is not tolerated, they do not look to set people up for failure. In fact, they glorify their heroes even more if they have battled against significant odds and eventually triumphed. Lance Armstrong, the American professional cyclist, remained a relatively obscure figure in the USA even after winning the Tour de France in what was considered a sport of minority interest by the national media at the time. He sky rocketed to 'A' List stardom, signaled by his appearance on the Oprah Winfrey Show, after he fought and won his battle with cancer and then went on to win a record number of Tours. All the American public asks is that you work hard and have no unfair advantages in winning – do this and you deserve your rewards and place in the galaxy... forever! The Americans are devoted to their concept of the Hall of Fame. They have these for virtually every sport. Now if that's not celebrating success what is?

What is the role of the fans in all this?

The helplessness and disempowerment that many of them felt throughout this tournament was, at times, almost unbearable as the following submission on Lee Sharpe's World Cup Blog illustrates:

*"Come on everyone it's time to wake up. Until we brought on the young guns (Crouchie, Aaron, etc) the side was characterised by over-paid, un-fit, performing prima-donnas (Owen, Beckham, Rooney, Lampard, Terry etc). We played better with 10 than 11 and Rooney deserves never to wear another England shirt ever – his stamping in the crutch defines the true character of a footballing idiot... As far as the manager goes, the sooner he goes the better, a more uninspiring manager I have never seen. He got what he deserves. He did not have the guts to drop Beckham... a weak corner and a pathetic free kick was all he dismally contributed. I am glad we've all been put out of our agony of painful watching; just wish we could have been 'put down' during normal time."*

— C J Buxton

But what right did the fans have to expect anything from the players. Is it wrong for those not empowered to deliver success, in other words anyone except for the players, coaches and FA, to set standards for it?

The keys to keeping everyone happy – players, managers, media and fans have already been examined – common purpose, common visions and common expectations. Those nations that view their teams' performance as 'successful' demonstrate this synchronicity.

*"The secret of success is constancy of purpose."*

— Benjamin Disraeli

Interestingly, looking through the World's newspapers, it was plain to see that great national pride was displayed by the players considered the most successful – more so than personal pride, and the players were seen, quite literally, as 'of' the people rather than a separate group.

Let's take a look at the varying reactions around the globe to certain nations' view of their teams' performance at the World Cup in relation to the success factor...

Putting their country on the map of world footballing nations seems to have been the joint aim of both the squad and supporters of Trinidad and Tobago:

The team was greeted by screaming fans on their arrival home to an official welcome. They were given a motorcade to the national stadium where they were individually rewarded for making (Trinidad &Tobago) visible internationally.

Lamisi Dabire a Ghanaian fan claimed that:

*"I am sure we are the only country to have celebrated so much after crashing out of the tournament. Our gallant Black Stars returned to a wonderful reception. Fans thronged the airport tarmac to welcome our national heroes and a musical concert was held in their honour. The players and coaches were decorated by the president with the highest national award, the Order of the Star of the Volta."*

The goal had been to represent Africa and to play well, success on both scores.

After more than 30 years of civil war the people of Angola were looking for something positive to cheer about. Fans were celebrating the fact that their team was participating at such a marvelous tournament. It was said that the positive atmosphere that pervaded throughout the nation did much to encourage a national reconciliation.

However, in Togo, following the fiasco over pay and conditions, whilst fans waited at the airport in Lome to welcome their players home with open arms the team were nowhere to be found. Some players returned secretly and others did not return at all. Was this an example of differing views on success- the fans were just happy to have their team participate, the players felt they had gained little for themselves or could it be that success for the players was finding a better life in Europe? Who knows!

In Ukraine football united the nation as millions of Ukrainians cheered their team on often watching matches outdoors in the pouring rain on specifically erected big screens. Andriy Hunder, a fan described how:

*"Thousands of fans greeted the players' arrival back home with flowers and champagne at Kiev's airport."*

Another country with a troubled past that was able to turn its' attentions away from the gloom at home for a while.

Italy's World Cup winning squad paraded through Rome with their trophy, in front of thousands of fans. Their first appointment was a meeting with President Giorgio Napolitano and Prime Minister Romano Prodi. The players then traveled by open-top bus to the Circus Maximus, where they showed off the World Cup trophy. With an estimated 500,000 supporters packing the streets of Rome, it took the bus hours longer than expected to fight it's way through the throngs and reach the Circus Maximus. Captain Fabio Cannavaro held the trophy aloft as his team mates joined in with a rendition of Queen's 'we are the champions' the ubiquitous football celebration anthem.

Yes, this is what celebration should be all about and the Italians did it in style.

Disappointed, but successful in reaching the final, the French squad arrived back and went straight to a lunch reception hosted by President Jacques Chirac. They had, after all, exceeded expectations that they'd get anywhere near this far.

Whilst examining the importance of celebrating success it is also worth having a look at the attitudes displayed towards failure.

Argentina could certainly believe at the beginning of the tournament that they had a squad that could go all the way. Losing to Germany was indeed a bitter blow. Yet the post match comments were telling:

Defender Gabriel Heinze *"I'm proud to be part of this group... we gave it all we had."*

Roberto Ayala *"We shouldn't be hard on ourselves. We can look ourselves in the mirror and go home proud of what we've done."*

The coach, Pekerman resigned after stating *"I can leave with my head held up high"* and despite the 'early' exit, a poll in an Argentine newspaper showed 73% of those polled wishing him to stay on as coach. This indicates that the coach was seen as successful in creating a team with an uplifting and inspiring style and brand of football. Argentina failed to reach the final and yet the supporters wanted more of this type of soccer. This suggests that how teams lose and how they play is important and can count towards the 'success' quota.

## Reasons to be cheerful

This book aims to provide a positive outlook and a reason for hope. In conclusion, let us reflect on the successes that England can lay claim to from this World Cup. We didn't find this an easy task and initially the only thing England seemed to succeed at was evading their fans and the press at Stansted airport on their return.

However, this difficulty in creating a list of successes may reflect the possibly unrealistic expectations we, the nation, had nursed of the England squad.

Were the team members being naïve in saying they could go all the way? Did they over estimate their own abilities unrealistically? Certainly post competition Neville and Gerrard both made mention that "we just weren't good enough". Did the press inflate them? The media, after all, wishes to sell newspapers and the high drama of missed opportunities and dashed dreams is a greater draw than mediocrity.

In hindsight, what might success have looked like?

By setting the bar at a realistic level for the future and seeking to bridge the gap with fans to ensure expectations are in line across the board, we can then start our rebuild. Taking time to celebrate the milestones along the way, there is no reason to believe that we cannot once again be a powerful force to contend with. These milestones could be the establishment of a new squad with clear goals based on a common vision and common purpose, this in turn would be communicated to the public so we have some idea of the direction we are moving in; the development of a team spirit through team building activity - frequent interaction among players between internationals; focus on solid, polished performance without panic and stress over results; a consistent improvement; contingency planning; the list goes on.

*"I know the price of success: dedication, hard work and an unremitting devotion to the things you want to see happen"*

— Frank Lloyd Wright

Let's tone down the hype a bit. As Martin Jol pointed out, *"Wayne Rooney was built up to an unhealthy extent before the tournament…despite arriving at the World Cup injured. It's unhealthy to heap so much on an individual player."*

Instead let's look for and celebrate examples of team excellence:

Let's celebrate when we achieve two or three tactical play combinations with which we feel comfortable. Again Jol highlighted that "the successful teams at the World Cup had tactical flexibility".

France and Italy both used negative comments from the press to gain motivation and leverage on their own game. Perhaps comments made by Sir Bobby Robson that the England team lacked hunger to succeed could be used to motivate them creating the right hunger for success. Let's create that hunger now by treating every game the England team plays not as an experiment or a 'friendly' try-out but as a game we play to win and to win convincingly! We must nurture a reputation for being a winning team, and make being 'an also ran' a thing of the past.

Let us leave you with what we consider to be some England triumphs from the last World Cup. We hope you will share our view of these as true successes:

- Owen Hargreaves, who had been booed when he had first appeared, won over his doubters with a splendid showing at the World Cup finals as he won the Man of the Match award for the penalty shoot-out defeat to Portugal.
- England's defence performed admirably throughout the competition conceding only two goals in five matches. Rio Ferdinand, in particular, received much praise from all quarters for his performances.

*"Our own Rio Ferdinand had a great tournament"*

— Gary Lineker

- Aaron Lennon, although only 19 years of age, made a spirited contribution when he took over from Beckham during the game against Portugal.
- England v Portugal (BBC Sport) "(England) battled on bravely for the rest of normal time (after Rooney's departure) and extra time with 10 men to take the game to a shoot out"

*"Roared on by England fans (the team) finally showed the passion and heart for a battle so often missing in this World Cup campaign"*

— (BBC Sport)

Observers agree that it was only when the England team reached a crisis point in the match against Portugal, with Sven's tactical formation in ruins and their talismanic 'best' player red-carded, that they then started to play some of their best football of the tournament. Facing defeat and down to 10 men seemed to release a level of intensity and concentration in their play, urgency, accuracy, purposeful aggression which had only been seen previously in the first 20 minutes of England's very first game in the tournament against Paraguay.

*"It's the English mentality. You pick yourself up and you fight back. You don't give anything away. England always go again. What else can we do? You can't give in and say 'that's it, we are going to stop playing football."*

— Gary Neville

A final comment on the England Fans from FA Chairman Geoff Thompson:

*"Throughout the whole tournament, England's fans have lived up to their reputation of being the best in the world…The fans turned each stadium England played in into a theatre of colour and cauldron of noise - an atmosphere the players enjoyed playing in…They brought life, colour and tremendous enthusiasm to every stadium and city that we visited."*

It is our hope that these fans, ourselves included, have many more reasons in the future to celebrate and rejoice in our England football team.

*"I have learned that success is to be measured not so much by the position that one has reached in life as by the obstacles which he has overcome while trying to succeed."*

— Booker T.Washington (1856-1915)

## Chapter 17:

# Back to the future

### Soccer City Stadium

### Johannesburg, SA

### Sunday July 11th 2010

Beyond the shimmering stadium, out into the steamy night and over the airwaves, the commentators and professional pundits drooled, a constant ooze of superlatives and clichés in the world's tongues, straining to give form and meaning to what the football universe had just witnessed:

*"A lesson in real class, bearing comparison with the team of 1966 and ..."*

*"Total Futbol, total!"*

*"What vision, what purpose and values, what iron will and self-belief in this team ....which has carried them all the way through this tournament!"*

*"...the free-flowing, expressive, attacking style of the 'New' England,"*

*"Incroyable, formidable, c'est superbe..."*

*"...the amazing way they adapted their play during the course of this game, really inspiring and a lesson in winning for every sportsman or woman"*

*"The head coach must be really proud of his team, the way they've come through and achieved their dream. The way they've kicked on from and exceeded the achievements of qualifying for this World Cup tournament, which some sceptics – myself included, had put down to luck, but now appears to be part of a bigger master plan..."*

*"Team dynamics, winning formulas, tactical flexibility in offence and defence, they all seem to move as one unit, gelling as a team..."*

*"Il Catennacio Inglese, una squadra meravigliosa, megagalactica!"*

*"...some would say, unconventional, techniques in the training camps, the use of sports psychology and motivational coaching, new methods of group motivation including affirmations and innovative team visualisations, techniques for life balance, the contract with the fans... now every team on the planet will want to study these techniques and learn how they can improve their own game!"*

*"Kunst durch Technik..."*

Below the commentary boxes and away from the glare of the flood-lit pitch, immediately behind the dug-out, the England coaching solutions team - Barnett, Palmer and Simpson, sat gazing on the wild bacchanalia before them and smiled at each other knowingly. Beside them on the bench lay a book, a faded and well-used copy of 'They thought it was all over....they were right!!', which, prior to kick-off, the whole England squad had personally autographed with glowing tributes to their contribution to the team's success.

Meanwhile, in Buckingham Palace, the Queen smiled into the camera as she announced that Monday would be a public holiday to celebrate the victorious homecoming of the England team from South Africa.

In the Houses of Parliament, the Speaker moved a vote of thanks in appreciation of the England team's outstanding success in the World Cup. The Prime Minister rose and amidst unanimous applause on both sides of the House, proposed a Knighthood for the England head coach and OBE's for every member of the squad.

Out in the suburbs and across the green land, crowds gathered to dance, sing, clap, party, play, laugh, embrace, make love, chant the names of their heroes:

*"We've won the World Cup!"*

*"Champions, champions, champions"*

*"There's only one Stevie Gerrard, one Stevie Gerr-ard, there's only one......"*

*"Sing when you're winning, we only sing when we're..."*

*"Football's coming home"*

*"We are the Champions......of the WORLD"*

*"England, England, E-N-G-L-A-N-D!"*

And so into that Night of Nights...

**They thought it was all over, they were wrong...**

**It is just beginning!**

# The Authors

**Jo Simpson** is a Professional Speaker, Facilitator and Executive Leadership Coach, who specialises in the area of the impact that mindset has on performance and team transformation. Jo has been running one of the most successful and respected Coaching and Mentoring Businesses in Dubai, UAE for the last 5 years working with clients that include KPMG, Lloyds Bank Plc, Barclays Bank, Microsoft, L'Oreal, Nokia and Gas and Oil Companies. Jo has recently made an 'intuitive' decision to relocate to the UK, while continuing to work on an international basis.

Jo is a Certified Professional Coach, whose interest in football began at an early age under the influence of her football-focused father and brother. It is a combination of this interest and her passion for people development, which led Jo to co-author this book. To find out more, or book Jo for speaking events and corporate leadership and team coaching visit www.josimpson.com / www.coachme.ae

**Ged Palmer** currently lives and works in Abu Dhabi in the United Arab Emirates as an International Human Resources Development Specialist. He is a psychologist, an expert in competency and performance management and a qualified coach who likes to work with organisations in bringing out their true talents and capabilities. He has been closely involved in team-building and leadership training for major multinationals such as bp and Total helping to build high performance work teams.

When not training for triathlons or performing as a musician with traditional Irish band, Inis Oirr (visit www.inis-oirr.com) Ged can be found at his home in Italy where he helps in the restoration and maintenance of a medieval castle. He is a life-long Liverpool football fan.

**Janice Barnett** is a coach, team builder, entrepreneur, writer and trainer with a lifelong passion for personal development and an unrelenting desire to turn her dreams into realities. Previously a diplomat working in international law enforcement she now runs her own coaching practice (www.pathfinderscoaching.net) and creative arts and activity centre in Burgundy where she now lives (www.thereallybigdreamcompany.com).

First and foremost though, Janice is an Arsenal supporter. Since watching Arsenal beat Wolves 2-1 back in 1977 with her Dad she hasn't looked back. Her most treasured moment is standing at Anfield with her sister watching the double winning match. A triumph of self-belief over the odds if ever there was one. However, there have been football lows – Janice had her arm broken whilst playing 6 a-side football for her office team. But to prove every cloud has a silver lining, this happened two days before the 1990 World Cup kicked off ensuring four weeks of uninterrupted football viewing.

Lightning Source UK Ltd.
Milton Keynes UK
15 May 2010

154201UK00001B/52/P

9 781905 823796